OVERKILL

GREGG OLSEN
AND
REBECCA MORRIS

TABLE OF CONTENTS

OVERKILL 1

ABOUT THE AUTHORS 5
INTRODUCTION BY GREGG OLSEN AND REBECCA MORRIS 7

HER LOVER'S WIFE (COLORADO) 9

THE TRIUMVIRATE: BOULDER, LITTLETON AND AURORA 13
MOUNTAINS OF TRAGEDY BY STEPHANIE COOK 14
HER LOVER'S WIFE 37
THE AMISH SERIAL KILLER 42
THE SON WHO BLEW UP THE NIGHT 52
CONFESSIONS OF A BITCH ON WHEELS 61
PHOTO ARCHIVE 79

THE DEADLY DAUGHTER-IN-LAW (ARIZONA) 93

THE FOURTH WIFE 97
FREED—BUT ARE THEY INNOCENT? 112
THE VICIOUS VIXEN BY STEPHANIE COOK 126
THE DEADLY DAUGHTER-IN-LAW 143
THE FOOTBALL BOOSTER 149
PHOTO ARCHIVE 157

FUNDAMENTAL LOVE (UTAH) 171

BABY KILLER 175
DEADLY DISTRACTION 182
THE LEGO MURDER 192
FUNDAMENTAL LOVE 200
KILLED WHILE SHE SLEPT 209
"IF I DIE, IT MAY NOT BE AN ACCIDENT" 224
PHOTO ARCHIVE 240

About the Authors

GREGG OLSEN is the *New York Times* bestselling author of twenty books, both true crime and fiction, including *Shocking True Story, Fear Collector, A Twisted Faith, Starvation Heights,* and *If Loving You Is Wrong.*

REBECCA MORRIS is the author of *Ted and Ann – The Mystery of a Missing Child and Her Neighbor Ted Bundy,* and *Bad Apples – Inside the Teacher/Student Sex Scandal Epidemic.*

Together they are the authors of *If I Can't Have You – Susan Powell, Her Mysterious Disappearance and the Murder of Her Children,* and the *New York Times* bestselling *Bodies of Evidence,* the first book in the Notorious USA series.

Introduction
By Gregg Olsen and Rebecca Morris

WE'VE WRITTEN ABOUT DOZENS OF CRIMES in our Notorious USA series. We've looked at the worst of the worst—husbands who killed their wives; women who killed their boyfriends; children who died because they became inconvenient to a parent's lifestyle; boys who took a weapon to school; love triangles that have turned ugly. How could they not?

What have we learned? Mental illness is often a factor, but most people who commit horrific acts do so because of jealousy or greed. It's alarming how many kill in order to collect on life insurance—even on their children.

Overkill is a compilation of Notorious Colorado, Arizona and Utah.

Colorado's edition includes three of the country's most infamous crimes which all occurred in the same area of Colorado: the murder of JonBenet Ramsey, the Columbine school shooting, and the Aurora movie theater massacre. We also report on an Amish serial killer, a fatal attraction that led to a murder, and on a minister's wife whose illicit passion drove her to murder.

In Arizona's, we update several cases, including: a man suspected of marrying vulnerable women, then killing them; two infamous Arizona killers freed after decades in prison; television's "*it girl*" Jodi Arias; a woman who was her mother-in-law's worst nightmare; and a football mom who got a little too cozy with members of her son's high school team.

And in Utah's edition, we report on one of the most sensational and heartbreaking crimes we've come across—Megan Huntsman, the Utah mother who hid seven dead infants in a garage; a cold case that was finally solved by a child's Lego; the rogue Fundamentalist Mormon who thought it was his right to marry and rape young girls; the sad case of children dying in hot cars; the husband who ended years of lying with murder; and an update on the disappearance of Susan Cox Powell, the case we write about in our book *If I Can't Have You.*

Why are we fascinated *and* repelled by crime? To paraphrase the Chinese philosopher Xun Zi, every one of us is born with feelings of envy and hate. If we give in to them, we're led to violence and crime. The rest of us struggle and might come close to that proverbial line in the sand, but we don't cross it. But we're disgusted—and a little intrigued—by those who do.

If there's a notorious case you'd like us to write about – anywhere in the country – contact us.

Gregg@GreggOlsen.com
Rebecca@RebeccaTMorris.com

And find out more about the Notorious USA series at our website:

www.notorioususa.com

HER LOVER'S WIFE

GREGG OLSEN
AND
REBECCA MORRIS

Notorious
Colorado

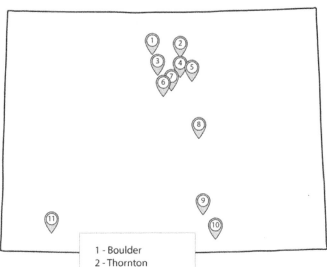

1 - Boulder
2 - Thornton
3 - Golden
4 - Denver
5 - Aurora
6 - Columbine
7 - Littleton
8 - Colorado Springs
9 - Walsenburg
10 - Trinidad
11 - Durango

The Triumvirate:
Boulder, Littleton and Aurora

BOULDER, LITTLETON AND AURORA, COLORADO SIT
in the foothills of the Rocky Mountains near Denver.

Central Colorado was settled by hunters, trappers,
farmers, and men mining silver and gold and the
merchants who did business with them. Millions of
years before, it was home to ancient glaciers, mountain
ranges, deserts, and even oceans and beaches.

The mines are long-closed and now the area is
known for its nature preserves, rock climbing, winter
sports, and what researchers call "quality of life."

The town of Nederland is a steep drive up the
southern side of the Rockies in an area called The Front
Range. It's just up the hill from Boulder, but motorists
climb a jaw-dropping 5,000 feet in just 17 miles. The
town of 1,500 people seems a world away from the
cluster of better-known towns down the hill, the
hometowns of JonBenet Ramsey, Columbine High
School, and the Century movie theater.

Together the towns form a tragic triumvirate of
western crime.

Mountains of Tragedy
By Stephanie Cook

I AM WRITING THIS A FEW DAYS AFTER MY 25th birthday, which means my family has spent a quarter of a century living in Colorado. We moved from sunny Burbank, California—where my parents grew up and met as high school sweethearts—to a tiny mountain town called Nederland when I was 22 days old. Despite the long winters, recent floods, and occasional feelings of isolation that mountain living can bring, my mom and dad, Sandy and Ted Cook, still live in the house they bought over the phone in 1989.

Colorado is renowned for its wild and mountainous beauty. In winter, trees glisten with snow. In summer, wildflowers adorn rivers and streams that reflect the clear blue skies above. The Front Range area, in particular, remains one of the most beautiful and safest places in the country to live and raise a family. I grew up wandering around my small mountain town with my two sisters, worrying only about mountain lions, bobcats, and bears, not strangers or guns. Strangers were always kind to me (and there were so few of them in Nederland anyway), and guns were for hunting pheasant and elk.

My dad keeps his guns locked and displayed in a glass cabinet in the living room. Growing up, I would watch him clean them before one of his hunting trips. As a child, I never thought much about it. Later, I wondered if the shooting at Columbine High School—and other mass shootings—changed his opinion about owning guns, especially as a father of three.

Over the past twenty years, I've watched three of America's greatest tragedies unfold—all clustered within miles of my house. The murder of JonBenet Ramsey left Boulder's tight-knit community longing endlessly for answers and justice, and the nearby towns of Aurora and Littleton lost dozens of people—most under the age of 30—to outbursts of gun violence carried out by angry and troubled young men.

The sun still shines in the Rockies, but the specters of the murder of JonBenet Ramsey, the shooting at Columbine High School, and the mass shooting at a movie theater in Aurora linger in the air like fog hanging over the Flatiron Mountains.

JonBenet Ramsey was a year younger than me. It's hard to believe the six year old imprinted in our minds as a child beauty contestant would be in her mid-twenties now. She grew up in Boulder, a picturesque university town. Many people who live in Nederland work and spend most of their time in Boulder—my family included—so JonBenet and I were essentially two little girls growing up at the same time in the same place. Still, when I first saw her image flash across the evening news, I thought she looked like she'd come from another planet. I was a mountain girl with bangs and pigtails, and she was a pageant star with a sash and a tiara.

Television news showed the same clip over and over of JonBenet prancing around on stage and singing "Cowboy's Sweetheart" in a tiny pink and white cowgirl outfit, complete with Texas-sized hair and full makeup. In all areas of life—not just child beauty pageants—the Ramseys' were successful. JonBenet's father, John, founded and presided over a computer services company. In 1996, his company grossed a billion dollars and he was named Entrepreneur of the Year by the Boulder Chamber of Commerce. John, JonBenet's mother Patsy, their nine-year-old son Burke, and JonBenet seemed to live a picture-perfect life. They owned a lavish 7,240 square foot, five bedroom home in one of Boulder's nicest neighborhoods and regularly hosted and attended parties with Boulder's social elite.

Our mothers took us to the same pediatric clinic. My mother remembers that after JonBenet's murder, the building was so overrun with investigators and reporters she couldn't get me in for my usual checkup. When we were six, both of us asked for the American Girl doll named Samantha. With long, dark hair, she looked more like me than JonBenet. American Girl describes Samantha as a bit of a tomboy and rule breaker, but all heart. Like JonBenet, she's in costume, but hers is a long dress that a girl would wear at the turn of the 20th century.

Boulder's most famous Santa Claus figured in both our lives. Patsy Ramsey hired Bill McReynolds, who worked as a mall Santa, for her Christmas party three years in a row. According to the Denver Post, Patsy loved how the Santa impersonator sprinkled gold glitter into his beard. My mother said I saw the same Santa at a mall right before JonBenet's death. "I remember because it was the best Santa we'd ever seen. You noticed how good his beard was," my mother told me.

Santa would soon be one of several suspects in JonBenet's murder.

The little girl, who was described as "the sparkplug of the family" disappeared sometime between Christmas night and the following morning. When John

Ramsey found his daughter's body, I was miles away playing with toys and eating egg bagels with my grandmother, who we were visiting in Palm Springs, California.

The Ramseys spent Christmas evening with friends, returning home around 9:30 p.m. John took JonBenet to her bed on the second floor, took off her shoes, and let Patsy undress her for bed. Meanwhile, Burke and his dad stayed up late assembling a Christmas toy. Eventually, John and Patsy went to bed in their third floor master bedroom. The family planned to leave for their Lake Michigan vacation home early the following day.

Around 5 a.m. Patsy woke up and headed downstairs to the kitchen. On the staircase she found a handwritten, three-page ransom note. The note addressed John Ramsey by his first name several times and demanded a payment of $118,000 in order to secure JonBenet's safe return. The ransom amount seemed odd not only because it was so specific, but also because John Ramsey had recently received a bonus of the same amount.

Despite threats in the letter that JonBenet would be beheaded should the Ramseys contact police, Patsy dialed 911 around 6 a.m., frantically explaining that she'd found a ransom note and her little girl gone.

The Ramseys' called some of their close friends, who the police allowed in and out of the house throughout the morning. Police searched the large house and found a broken window near the basement. John Ramsey said he'd broken the window about a year earlier after locking himself out of the house, but authorities suspected this may have provided an entrance point for an intruder.

While one lone detective waited hours for backup, she directed John Ramsey and a friend to search the house for anything seemingly out of place. Around 1:30 p.m.—nearly eight hours after they discovered her missing—John Ramsey found his daughter lying in a small, windowless room in a corner of the basement. Her body was covered in a white blanket, and her favorite Barbie nightgown was beside her body. Cord had been loosely tied around her wrist. A garrote—made with cord tied in intricate knots to the broken handle of one of Patsy's paintbrushes—was around the girl's throat. The ligature was sunk deep into JonBenet's skin. Her white long johns were stained with urine and blood. Strange marks on JonBenet's back resembled those made by a Taser gun. During the autopsy it became clear that the right side of JonBenet's skull was severely fractured after a hit by a blunt object. It also appeared that JonBenet had suffered some type of trauma to her genitals, although no semen was found. The coroner listed the cause of death as "asphyxia by strangulation associated with craniocerebral trauma."

It was a brutal end for a little girl who seemed to be living a charmed life. Little Miss Colorado 1995 was buried in a tiara in her parent's hometown of Marietta, Georgia.

The investigation of her murder created tension between Boulder Police, the FBI, and the District Attorney's Office—and between law enforcement and the Ramseys'.

As one journalist pointed out, news coverage of the murder could only be compared to 1932's Lindbergh kidnapping. Media from all over the world descended on Boulder. Network television crews came to town, and *People, Newsweek,* and *The National Inquirer* churned out glossy spreads on the slain pageant princess. Images of her singing and dancing flooded cable news.

Local grocery stores wrapped paper around the covers of newspapers and magazines to shield children from seeing crime scene photos (and eventually, autopsy photos).

Was there a killer on the loose? The mayor of Boulder said no—which sent a signal that the police were focusing on the family. The police encouraged the media to focus on the Ramseys', too.

Over and over, photos and videos of the young child in full pageant regalia haunted the airwaves. For many people there was something very dark and even neglectful about parading a little girl in front of the world wearing the makeup and clothes of someone several times her age. Many saw it as a child being sexualized.

Within days of the murder, the Ramseys' were known as "the most hated couple in America." What kind of people dress up a child in a tacky costume and big hair and makeup? Where Patsy Ramsey came from—the South—*good* parents did. There was a family tradition of beauty pageants. Patsy was Miss West Virginia 1977, as was JonBenet's aunt three years later. And as the Ramseys explained, Patsy was recovering from ovarian cancer and knew it could eventually kill her. She didn't think she'd be around to see JonBenet become a teenager, so the pageant experience was something the mother and daughter could share *now*. And the videos? A childhood event photographed for parents and grandparents, much like a Little League game or piano recital.

It seemed the Ramseys' couldn't do anything right. Within days of the murder they hired attorneys. When they hired a PR consultant—on the advice of their attorney, so he wouldn't have to field calls for interviews and could focus on the investigation—public sentiment turned against them again.

It was widely reported that John and Patsy refused to meet with the police. In fact, they both did. It was only after a family friend realized they were fast becoming suspects that they hired attorneys.

Many believe that local authorities were ill equipped to handle such a high-profile investigation. The town, and its police force, weren't experienced at investigating murders. JonBenet's was the only homicide in Boulder in 1996.

Police didn't know what to make of all of the contradictory evidence. It was unprecedented to find a ransom note, then discover a child dead in a house. Based on the floor plan of the home, an intruder would have had to pass a door leading outside to bring JonBenet down two floors to the cellar area. Which means she could have been taken out of the house, but wasn't. There was no follow up phone call asking for a ransom, and there were no prints in the fresh snow outside the home, although, as one reporter clarified later, there were only patches of snow and it didn't reach each doorway.

Things just weren't adding up.

While the Ramseys remained under a microscope, other leads into the intruder theory surfaced and then fizzled. Remember the Santa that Patsy hired, Bill McReynolds? A former professor at the University of Colorado, he was said to have taken a liking to JonBenet. Earlier that Christmas season he'd given her a note, saying that Santa would give her a special gift after Christmas. As authorities investigated McReynolds they found odd links between him and JonBenet. McReynolds' own daughter had been abducted exactly 22 years to the day before JonBenet's murder. On top of that, McReynolds' wife wrote a play about a young girl being molested and murdered in a basement prior to JonBenet's murder. Investigators ruled him out based on hair and handwriting samples. When my mother found out that I, too, may have met that Santa, and that we employed his son to work on our computers at home, she got a little freaked out.

Other neighbors and Ramsey friends were eventually ruled out as well, and the years rolled by with little progress and lots of frustration. In 1999, a Boulder grand jury indicted both John and Patsy on two counts each of child abuse resulting in death in connection with the first-degree murder of their daughter. The charges didn't directly accuse the Ramseys of killing their daughter—instead it meant they had permitted her to be in a dangerous situation. But Boulder District Attorney Alex Hunter refused to prosecute. The sealed indictment wasn't made public until 2013.

Legally, very little has happened in JonBenet's case since the 1990s. Patsy Ramsey died in 2006, and that same year authorities thought they had a break. A former teacher named John Mark Karr confessed to killing JonBenet, and authorities brought him from Thailand back to the U.S. for questioning. He was later cleared when his DNA didn't match and relatives explained he'd been in Georgia—not Colorado—that Christmas. In 2008, Boulder District Attorney Mary Lacy publicly exonerated each of the Ramseys and apologized to them when a Touch DNA test showed that neither of them matched the evidence found on JonBenet's clothing the night of the murder.

Still, suspicion continues to lurk. The most popular theories I hear are either that Patsy, an uptight stage mom, killed JonBenet in a fit of rage, or that JonBenet's brother, Burke, had hurt his sister either by accident or on purpose, and his parents staged the crime scene as a cover-up.

There are some twenty books about the murder, including two by John Ramsey, who has remarried. Most of them rehash what few facts there are, and the investigation, widely viewed as bungled.

Technically, the Ramseys are in the clear, but go to Boulder and you'll still find that everyone has a theory on what happened in the brick Tudor on 15th street.

Still, life has gone on. In 2011, Gallup named Boulder "The Happiest Town in America."

JONBENET'S MURDER SHOWED US HOW TRAGIC A SINGLE DEATH CAN BE IN A TIGHT-KNIT COMMUNITY LIKE BOULDER. Nothing could have prepared residents of Colorado's Front Range area for the massacre of dozens of people —many of them in their teens and twenties—in two of America's deadliest shootings.

It was just after 11 a.m. on a warm April day in Littleton when Eric Harris and Dylan Klebold pulled up to Columbine High School. They'd missed morning classes and in a few minutes, the lunch bell would ring and hundreds of classmates would swarm to the cafeteria. Brooks Brown, a student who was once tormented by Eric but had since made peace with him, happened to step outside for a smoke and see the boys.

"What's the matter with you?" Brooks asked. "We had a test in Psychology."

"It doesn't matter anymore," Eric told him."Brooks, I like you. Get out of here. Go home. Now!"

Brooks shrugged and walked off, leaving the school and the danger that loomed behind.

I remember that Tuesday morning, April 20, 1999. I was nine and in elementary school, and my sister was 13 and an eighth grader at the middle/senior high school in Nederland. My mother picked me up early that day and on the car radio we heard reports of a possible hostage situation at Columbine High School. By the time we arrived home, the story was being reported live on television. We watched as streams of students literally ran for their lives in a line, holding their hands over their heads, then rushed to find their friends or parents in the crowd outside. In some images, a white sheet covered up something—or someone—on the grass. A few of the fleeing kids spoke to reporters, frantically explaining how the girl hiding under a desk near them got shot and two guys were throwing bombs and laughing at people. Students mentioned that the gunmen wore black trench coats and might be part of a gang of students called the "trench coat mafia." Meanwhile, kids were still inside the school and so were the gunmen.

Live coverage of the shooting was interrupted as President Clinton made a brief statement. He said his prayers were with the people of Littleton, and that he'd have more to say as details of the situation emerged. Both local and national news broadcasts followed the breathtaking situation unfolding. In one of the most dramatic moments televised live, a bloodied boy dangled halfway out of a shattered second story window. One of his legs seemed limp and he looked like a ragdoll as he forced himself out through the broken glass. Suddenly, a group of SWAT team members jumped on one of their vehicles and grabbed the boy. It was a harrowing rescue that offered the first glimpse at what might be going on inside that school. The boy in the window would be the last seriously injured person to leave the building alive. He was named class valedictorian the next year.

Hours after the first shots rang out, the SWAT team finally entered the school. When they made their way to the library they found dozens of injured and dead students, including Eric Harris and Dylan Klebold who had committed suicide.

Those lost hours were precious and devastating. The only adult killed that day, teacher and coach Dave Sanders, lay bleeding to death for four hours. Sanders, along with two custodians, ran to the cafeteria when the shooting began to warn students and lead them out an exit. After Sanders was shot, he laid on the floor in a science room where students used articles of their clothing to stop his bleeding and made a gurney out of table legs. A sign reading "1 bleeding to death" was posted in the window, and one of the teachers gave police regular updates on Sanders' condition. But help didn't come until it was too late for the basketball coach, father, and husband, whose dying words were of his daughters: *"Tell my girls I love them."*

Teenagers opening fire in school was almost unprecedented. It had happened before, but this was the first time Americans watched and listened, united in horror. Reporters, faced with filling a live broadcast and trying to give America some answers as to what was unfolding, began clinging to details recalled by students as they escaped. Word spread about the trench coat mafia and soon a description emerged of the boys as racist loners who were bullied by jocks and wanted revenge.

"If you saw someone walking around in a trench coat, people were freaked out," my older sister Noele remembers. Those assumptions stuck, and for years to come people in Colorado and around the country thought they knew what had happened.

We were all wrong.

It wasn't just jocks that got shot that morning—it was anyone who got in the way of a bullet. Eric Harris and Dylan Klebold killed 12 students and one teacher, and injured more than twenty others. Aside from attending the same high school, the only thing everyone had in common was simply bad luck. Outside, the boys shot at anyone who moved and inside they taunted and shot peers at random. The truth is, the boys didn't just want to kill certain students. They wanted to kill everyone and everything.

Harris and Klebold weren't really bullied loners. True, they didn't like jocks and hated a lot of the kids at school, but both had friends and attended school functions. The boys—who referred to themselves by the nicknames Vodka (Dylan) and Reb (Eric)—were two very different people with very different reasons to act violently.

Dylan Klebold was a bright—and depressed—young man. His journal, which was released years after the shooting along with thousands of other documents left by the boys, is a combination of philosophical ranting and teenage heartache. In the beginning, he rambles about the shallowness of others and the pain of seeing the world differently from his peers. He writes about how devastated and betrayed he felt after his closest friend began spending all of his time with a new girlfriend. Eventually he writes that he's fallen deeply in love and thinks he may have found his soul mate. He is later crushed to find that the girl barely noticed him.

Despite a good family and some academic success, Dylan saw failure in everything he did. He contemplated suicide and felt immense pain and loneliness.

Where Dylan was sensitive to a fault, Eric, also a bright young man, seemed to feel nothing: no love, no sorrow, just pure hate and loathing. Dylan saw himself as a total loser, but not Eric. Eric believed he was better and smarter than everyone else. He drew swastikas, wrote about how inferior women would always be to men, and scratched the words "KILL MANKIND" in huge letters in his journal. Hate was Eric's mantra, and more than anything he wanted to be feared by those around him. But people took to Eric. He could be charming, and he used that talent to attract and manipulate people.

In addition to offering a window into the boys' psyche, the released documents revealed how much worse Columbine was *supposed* to be.

The fact that Columbine is remembered as a shooting, rather than a bombing, is a fluke. The plan was to carry out the attack on April 19th—the anniversary of the Oklahoma City Bombing—not the 20th. Klebold and Harris meant to set off another massive bombing—with some shooting tossed in.

If things had gone as planned, a bomb would have exploded in a park a few miles from the school to distract authorities. Then, as Eric had carefully calculated, just as the flow of students through the cafeteria peaked—right around the lunch bell—the real bomb would go off. That explosion could have killed hundreds of students. The guns would allow the boys to shoot at survivors as they ran. This, the boys figured, would be the fun part. Finally, as first responders surrounded the school and reporters flocked, the boys' two cars, both filled with explosives, would detonate on live television.

It was a plan Eric and Dylan spent almost a year and a half on. For some reason it failed. None of the bombs went off. Eric and Dylan were puzzled, and decided to go ahead and open fire. They started at the top of the stairs outside the cafeteria, patrolled the halls, threw pipe bombs, and made their way to the library, where they taunted and tormented people hiding under desks, killing them at random.

Just as much of Boulder and America believed John and Patsy Ramsey had killed their daughter or covered up her murder, there was and is widespread bias against the parents of Eric Harris and Dylan Klebold. How could they *not* know their sons were writing angry missives in their journals, drawing plans to bomb their school, buying guns, and stockpiling ammunition?

The parents of Eric Harris haven't said much, but in an article in "O Magazine" in 2009, Sue Klebold wrote of the "indescribable grief and shame" she has lived with since the 1999 tragedy.

In the weeks and months that followed the killings, I was nearly insane with sorrow for the suffering my son had caused, and with grief for the child I had lost. But while I perceived myself to be a victim of the tragedy, I didn't have the comfort of being perceived that way by most of the community. I was widely viewed as a perpetrator or at least an accomplice since I was the person who had raised a 'monster.'

In one newspaper survey, 83 percent of respondents said that the parents' failure to teach Dylan and Eric proper values played a major part in the Columbine killings.

Eventually, after reading his journals, Sue Klebold decided Dylan intended to kill himself that day. Since then she has tried to educate herself—and help others—dealing with the suicide of a loved one.

The Columbine shooting changed school safety across the country, in both positive and negative ways. Parents, school counselors, and teachers began to take student bullying and depression more seriously and some schools implemented emergency techniques and drills. In other ways though, schools responded with policies that may have made matters worse. Under a zero tolerance policy toward potential weapons, a student accidentally wearing a coat with a sharp snowboarding tool in it, or a parent accidentally leaving a butter knife in a student's lunchbox, was grounds for suspension or expulsion. In 2013, a Maryland second-grader was suspended from school for chewing a Pop-Tart into the shape of a gun.

Students were confused—should they report a peer's violent joke, or not?

My older sister remembers random locker searches taking place after Columbine. They may have prevented other crimes, but they diminished the sense of trust between students and administrators.

Meanwhile, our country now looks for a boogyman who could appear anywhere: an angry young man with a gun opening fire in places where we used to feel safe, like a school or a mall movie theater.

JESSICA GHAWI'S FIRST BRUSH WITH GUN VIOLENCE left her with an eerie feeling.

She had just left the food court at Toronto's Eaton Centre shopping mall on June 2, 2012 when a 23-year old man opened fire, killing two other young men and wounding five.

"I can't get this odd feeling out of my chest. This empty, almost sickening feeling won't go away," Jessica (who went by the last name of Redfield on her blog) wrote a few days later. The 24-year old sports writer had recently moved from San Antonio to Denver and was visiting Toronto when a normal trip to the mall for sushi turned into a sickeningly close brush with danger. Jessica learned that three minutes after she left the food court, a gunman stood where she'd just finished eating, and shot seven people.

She took to her personal blog to write about the incident, writing in the final paragraph:

> *I feel like I am overreacting about what I experienced. But I can't help but be thankful for whatever caused me to make the choices that I made that day. My mind keeps replaying what I saw over in my head. I hope the victims make a full recovery. I wish I could shake this odd feeling from my chest. The feeling that's reminding me how blessed I am. The same feeling that made me leave the Eaton Center. The feeling that may have potentially saved my life.*

Now, just a few weeks later, Jessica was back in Denver and back to her old self. She was on her way to a midnight movie, trading witty remarks with a friend on Twitter. When she entered the theater, did she get that "odd feeling" again?

July 20, 2012 was a busy night at the Century 16 multiplex in Aurora, Colorado. People on dates, celebrating birthdays, and hanging out with their families were in line for the 12:05 a.m. premiere of "The Dark Knight Rises," the latest Batman movie in which, once again, he protects Gotham City from a new menace.

Just as the movie began, a man walked in wearing head-to-toe black tactical clothing. His hair was dyed shocking orange. He rolled two tear gas grenades down the aisles and, according to witnesses, announced something like, "I am the Joker." (The Joker is the enemy of Batman.)

Was this some crazy promotion for the premiere? Maybe it was a college kid pulling a weird prank? Suddenly, smoke filled the theater, burning everyone's eyes and skin. Bullets sprayed the back row and several pierced the wall, killing three people in another theater. Then, the gunman fired at people running in the aisles. This was no elaborate hoax, movie plot, or publicity stunt —this menace was real.

Police first received a call about the shooting at 12:39 a.m., and by 12:45, they spotted a man wearing a mask outside the theater. At first, James Holmes seemed to be an officer dressed in tactical gear, but police quickly realized he was the gunman. Holmes made no effort to escape as officers detained him.

Inside, the dead and wounded were everywhere and ambulances were yet to arrive. Desperate to help the victims, police began transporting injured people in their vehicles. The carnage was massive: twelve people were killed—including Jessica Ghawi—and 70 others were wounded.

At Holmes' apartment building, his neighbor wasn't getting any sleep. Loud music had been blaring from the apartment since around midnight, and the neighbor decided to at least give him a warning before she called the police. When she went to his apartment, the door seemed to be unlocked, but rather than enter she decided to call police. Little did she know, she'd just avoided a deadly trap.

He had booby-trapped the apartment. It was just what the Joker himself would have done: get caught at a shooting, let authorities search the house, and then bang!, round two of the terror unfolds. His idea to lead authorities into a potential explosion was eerily similar to what Dylan and Eric had planned at Columbine. Luckily, Holmes also failed at causing an even bigger disaster as a bomb squad successfully navigated the trap.

Coloradans again groped for a way to deal with a massacre that shattered their sense of safety. The gun lobby geared up. Activists spoke out. Newspapers published editorials.

During the 13 years between Columbine and Aurora, mass shootings spread across the nation, as if contagious. At Virginia Tech, a 23-year-old student gunned down 56 people on campus; in an Omaha mall, a 19-year-old man killed and wounded 13 people; at a Tucson meet and greet for Rep. Gabrielle Giffords, a 22-year-old man killed and wounded 19 people, including Giffords, who was shot in the head but recovered.

Over and over, gun violence took lives, but gun laws remained relatively unchanged on a national level.

I asked my father if the shooting had changed his opinions on gun ownership. He said he was obviously more aware of public shootings, but it didn't change his mind about owning guns.

"I'm just one of those people who would want to protect my own," he said. "If you guys were at school and I heard something going on, I'd probably grab my gun and go try and help. I'd go to those extremes to protect my family," he told me.

He said background checks weren't enough to prevent gun sales to disturbed people. "These guys seem like they're pretty young and a lot of them don't have a record yet that would show up. I think the one thing that could help is regular background checks and if some kind of psych evaluation went with it."

Why do the citizens of Colorado continue to hold on to their guns after the tragedies they've seen unfold? Many seemed to side with the state's governor, John Hickenlooper, who said that anyone intent on harming others will find a way, gun laws or not.

James Holmes pleaded not guilty by reason of insanity to charges of killing 12 people and injuring 70. His trial is scheduled to take place in early 2015. The prosecution plans to seek the death penalty.

In October, 2014 the city of Aurora, Colorado released a report with recommendations it said it has already begun implementing, including training more SWAT paramedics. The report also recommends that theaters implement emergency procedures.

On December 14, 2012, five months after the shooting at the Aurora movie theater, 20-year-old Adam Lanza killed his mother—an avid gun collector—and then shot 20 students and 6 teachers at Sandy Hook Elementary School in Newtown, Conn. It was the deadliest mass shooting at a high school or grade school in U.S. history and second only to the 2007 Virginia Tech shooting as the deadliest mass shooting by a single person in U.S. history.

The perpetrators of all three shootings—Columbine, Aurora and Virginia Tech—had obtained semi-automatic weapons, some legally. The shootings prompted renewed debate about gun control, including proposals for making the background-check system universal, and for new federal and state legislation banning the sale and manufacture of certain types of semi-automatic firearms and magazines with more than ten rounds of ammunition. Another issue is the purchase of firearms by persons known to have mental health issues. All the young men were known to have mental health problems.

My dad's guns are still in the glass case in the living room. Today, my sister is raising two young boys who often make weekend trips to our parents' home. My father told me that he does one thing differently. He had always kept a cable woven through the guns inside the case, and locked, as an extra precaution, but with one gun and some ammunition left outside the cable in case of an intruder. Now, all of the guns are locked twice.

It's not a big change, but it's a sign that intruders are no longer the only threat striking fear in parents' hearts.

Afterword

AFTER A MAY, 2014 SHOOTING AT THE UNIVERSITY of California, Santa Barbara, which left six students dead from gun or knife wounds, parents and a few politicians questioned the federal government's response to earlier shootings.

"Have we learned nothing?" the father of one of the latest victims asked.

Apparently very little.

Americans—and Congress—remain conflicted about gun control.

After every mass shooting, there are new calls for gun control but little changes. Many believe Congress is afraid of the gun lobby, which contributes financially to political races.

In the year after the shooting at Columbine, 800 gun bills were introduced around the country. Less than 10 percent passed. One of the failed efforts included a federal bill to close the gun show loophole, which allows unlicensed dealers to sell guns without background checks. The mentally ill continue to find ways to buy guns.

In Colorado, there *have* been two significant changes. Background checks are now required for guns purchased at gun shows, and ammunition magazines are limited to 15 rounds.

Colorado's gun laws are seen as being middle-of-the road. They are less restrictive than those in New York or Massachusetts, where there are bans on assault weapons. They are more restrictive than those in states like Texas, which is known for being gun-friendly.

Yet it is Texas, home of more guns than people, passed a law holding adults criminally liable when a child or teenager has access to a gun.

After every mass shooting, gun owners argue for the right to carry guns in public places and applications for concealed weapons permits increase. As for the argument that there would be fewer mass shootings if, for example, teachers and principals or average citizens were armed, **there is little evidence that an armed onlooker has ever stopped a mass shooting.** An investigation by *Mother Jones* concluded that no more than 1.6 percent of mass shootings were ended by armed civilians. Retired or off-duty police officers are more likely to intervene.

The debate about passing stricter gun control laws is never as heated as immediately after a shooting. But interest falls off quickly.

After the Newton shooting, the Obama administration introduced proposals for universal background checks on gun sales and a new ban on assault weapons. Both failed.

In October, 2014, California became the first state in the country to allow private citizens to ask a court to seize guns from family members who they believe are potentially violent.

In November, 2014 Washington State became the seventh state requiring background checks on all sales and transfers.

STEPHANIE COOK is a free-lance writer based in Seattle. She was a reporter for the Durango Herald and was the news editor of the Fort Lewis College Independent, both in Durango, Colorado.

To read about one of the country's first school shootings, on February 2, 1996 in Moses Lake, Washington, see "The Boy Who Fired the First Shot," by Rebecca Morris and Gregg Olsen. It's a chapter in our book of the same title, and also in the New York Times bestselling collection, "Bodies of Evidence," both part of our Notorious USA series.

Her Lover's Wife

IT WAS SUPPOSED TO LOOK LIKE A ROBBERY GONE wrong.

On Sept. 12, 1990, a woman wearing camouflage fatigues and a ski mask surprised Dianne Hood, 32, as she left a community center in Colorado Springs, CO. As the person lunged for her purse, Hood screamed, "Take it!" But that wasn't what her attacker, Jennifer Reali, was after. She pulled out a .45 caliber Colt revolver and shot Hood. A witness to the murder described the scene:

> *"I saw her eyes and they were dark eyes and full of hate. She walked over to where Dianne was lying. Dianne was begging for her life, and she took very careful aim and shot her again."*

The cold-blooded murder of the mother of three on a patio outside Park Community Center, where Dianne Hood had been attending a lupus support meeting, shocked Colorado Springs. The community was shocked again when Jennifer Reali and Dianne Hood's husband, Brian Hood, were arrested two days later.

Now, nearly 25 years after the shooting, Colorado Springs is shocked again. Reali—who had been sentenced to life in prison for killing her lover's wife—has traded her cell for a half-way house.

SHE WAS DUBBED THE "FATAL ATTRACTION KILLER" after the 1987 movie, the film that may be responsible for scaring more men into monogamy than any Sunday morning sermon has. Michael Douglas has a one-night stand and lives to regret it when Glenn Close becomes a stalker and killer. Eventually she gets her comeuppance, but only after threatening his wife and child and making stew out of the family's pet rabbit.

Jennifer Reali met Brian Hood in the Jacuzzi at a health club. They were so lovey-dovey that other members of the fitness club thought they were a happy young couple. She was attractive, he was handsome and attentive.

They were married—but not to each other. Jennifer, who was 29, was married to Ben Reali, a career Army officer. She was the daughter of a Seattle architect and life in the Army wasn't at all what she was accustomed to.

Growing up, the pretty, light-haired young woman did well in school and traveled to France for her junior year in college. Family would later say that she had fought depression and loneliness much of her life. She cut short her education at the University of Washington in Seattle to marry Ben Reali, an Army captain.

After giving birth to two children, she continued to be depressed—and bored. She took to drinking a bottle of wine or a few beers each day. Ben was strict and emotionally abusive with her and the children. Jennifer was bored and felt trapped in her marriage.

She wasn't bored after meeting Brian Hood.

Brian Hood was an insurance salesman. He turned more than a few heads. He was tall, 6' 4" blonde, handsome, and confident. Brian had met Dianne as an undergraduate at Angelo State University in Texas, where he was a member of the football team. They were married in December 1980 and moved to Colorado Springs, where Brian eventually landed a job as a liquor salesman. In 1986, after joining Fellowship Bible Church and becoming a born-again Christian, Hood quit the liquor business and began selling life insurance. Dianne learned she had lupus, an immune-system disorder that sometimes proves fatal.

Brian told Jennifer, his Jacuzzi buddy and now lover, about Dianne's debilitating illness—and that he had a $100,000 life insurance policy that would pay double if she died accidentally. He concocted the crime, Jennifer claimed, because he hated his wife and didn't want to lose his three young children in a divorce.

TWO DAYS AFTER THE MURDER, JENNIFER REALI confessed.

She claimed she had been brainwashed by Brian, who had convinced her using biblical interpretations that God wanted his wife dead. The born-again Christian explained that it was God's will that his wife die—and that Jennifer should pull the trigger—and said she should think of it as a mercy killing. In other words, *divorce* would be a sin, but killing his wife would not be.

Hood denied orchestrating the murder, portraying himself as the victim of a fatal attraction. His lawyers contended that Reali acted alone, out of a crazed desire to get even because he had decided to break up with her.

Their separate trials titillated the town. Jennifer described how they had sex on top of her washing machine and in her Jeep Cherokee.

Jennifer Reali was sentenced to life in prison after being convicted of first-degree murder, despite the defense portrayal of her as a helpless pawn of Brian Hood's.

Brian Hood was convicted of second-degree murder for conspiring to kill his wife and was sentenced to 37 years in prison. He briefly escaped from the medium-security Fremont Correctional Facility in 1997 with another inmate, but was recaptured in less than 18 hours.

JENNIFER REALI IS IN HER EARLY 50S NOW. HER ONCE blonde hair has traces of gray and her face is a little fuller.

Her life sentence was commuted by former Gov. Bill Ritter in 2011, making her eligible for parole sooner. Her parole was denied later that year mostly because of opposition from Hood's family.

But in August, 2014 she was transferred to a halfway house in Lakewood. The prison system says she has had good behavior during her 24 years in prison. "I am not the woman I was 20 years ago," she said in a television interview.

But Darla Blue, Dianne Hood's friend, was shocked by Reali's release to the halfway house, even if she has spent more than two decades in prison.

"She had planned this out," she said of the murder. "The fact you have somebody capable of doing that, and following through with it? To me, whether you're on good behavior or not, it tells me the kind of person you are."

A spokesman for the former governor said the commutation brings Jennifer's punishment more closely in line with that of Brian Hood's. (As in other, similar, cases, she received a stiffer sentence than the man who convinced her to kill.)

Jennifer Reali was the mother of two children. Dianne Hood was the mother of three.

The five young children who lost their parents when one woman shot the other are adults now. Their lives are forever changed by a doomed fatal attraction.

The Amish Serial Killer

WHEN FIFTY-SIX YEAR OLD ELI STUTZMAN STABBED himself in a vein in his left arm and bled to death in 2007, he left no suicide note and no explanation or apology for his life and crimes. He'd been a husband, a father, a gay Amish man and a serial killer.

Several years after his suicide, he remains a suspect in the murders of two men in Durango, Colorado.

Eli, the fourth of thirteen children born to a "low-Amish" family in Ohio, members of the Swartzentruber Order, was trouble from childhood. He rebelled in some not uncommon ways—he secretly learned to drive, owned a radio, and began to smoke and drink. But then his actions went way beyond rebelling. He did drugs, had sex with women and men, and began to kill.

His pregnant wife, Ida, died in a mysterious fire on their Ohio farm in 1977 most likely set by Eli. Because they were Amish, her death wasn't aggressively investigated and was assumed to be accidental.

He may have strangled or smothered his nine-year-old son Danny. He admitted leaving the little boy, clad in blue pajamas, to freeze to death in a Nebraska ditch. He killed his gay roommate in Texas in 1985 and while on the run he lived near Durango, Colorado. That's when the still-unsolved murders of David Tyler and Dennis Slaeter occurred.

In December 1987, the law finally up to Stutzman. It had taken two years, but the nameless child found in the blue pajamas had finally been identified and police thought they knew who had killed him—his father.

The coroner believed Danny had been strangled or suffocated but couldn't prove it. Gut feelings told the investigators that they were dealing with a murder. Circumstances pointed that way, but they needed physical evidence. There was none.

Eli Stutzman was the subject of Gregg's first book, *Abandoned Prayers—An Incredible True Story of Murder, Obsession and Amish Secrets:*

INSIDE THE COURTHOUSE, STUTZMAN, IN JEANS AND flannel shirt, sat facing the spectators and attorneys; his face was ashen and his eyes rarely met the gaze of others. He looked the part of a spectator—a farmer or a mechanic or anyone else from the community. Word had sifted through the courtroom: Eli Stutzman was going to plead guilty and, more important, he was going to tell his story.

The legal rigmarole went quickly. County Attorney Dan Werner and defense attorney Bill Gallup had agreed Stutzman would plead guilty to the misdemeanors. Though there had been no plea bargain, Werner indicated that the state had agreed to dismiss without prejudice the child-abuse charge. As a part of the agreement, Stutzman would take the stand.

Gallup questioned him first.

"What was your son's condition when you left Wyoming? Had he been treated for any illness?"

"Yes."

"What?"

"He was on medication."

Stutzman explained that Dean and Margie Barlow had given him a prescription and told him how to administer the medication. Stutzman said he had mapped out a route to Ohio via U.S. 81. He said he took 80 at first.

"At some point in the trip, did you notice anything unusual about your son, at any point, or notice that he wasn't alert, or what happened if anything?"

"In the afternoon he complained a little bit about not feeling real good and I suggested stopping, not continuing, for seeing a doctor, and he said he just wanted to lay down and he would be fine."

Stutzman moved some luggage and toys in the car so that the boy would have room to stretch out.

"What eventually drew your attention to the back of the car?"

"Well, later, late in the evening, during the night— I believe it was time for his medication— I reached back while driving and got a hold of him and I couldn't get him awake."

Gallup looked concerned. "He didn't respond to touch?"

"Right. He did not respond. So I pulled over to a—to see what it was about. I was shocked to see that there was no response at all."

Gallup questioned Stutzman about his medical training, and the witness said that he had been a hospital orderly and knew the techniques of CPR and heart massage.

"So, then, would you relate to the judge what, if anything, you did when you found your son didn't respond to your touch?"

"I was shocked. I could not believe finding him that way."

"What did you do?"

"I—"

Gallup told him to speak up.

"I tried desperately to revive him."

Stutzman said that he tried mouth-to-mouth resuscitation and heart massage, but that nothing worked. The boy was dead, and Stutzman didn't know what to do. He was somewhere on U.S. 81, close to Chester, Nebraska. He drove to a place off the main road.

"I had difficulty facing the fact that he had died. I couldn't understand, couldn't figure out why he died, or would have died under the circumstances.

"I pulled off the main road and made another turn or two and found a place in a valley, up in a valley, where I thought there was nobody else around, and I spent some time, quite a bit of time there praying, and I tried again to revive him and I just—"

Gallup cut him off. "Did you think at any time that maybe this was due to the disfavor of your God for the way you had left the church? Was that something that was bothering you?"

The defendant shook his head. "No, I can't tell— I don't remember that crossing my mind, that I felt guilty because of my past in any way."

Stutzman thought he stayed in the valley for several hours, trying to figure out what to do with the body in the back of the Gremlin.

"I knew that I could go and try and, you know, find a phone and get an emergency squad, but I did have feelings that maybe the facts would be against me."

"What?"

"The facts would be against me from my family."

Stutzman's voice was so soft, Gallup again asked him to speak louder.

"I thought the fact about my family might be against me, that I was not taking proper care of him. I feared for that. .. and I had a big difficulty realizing what had happened and why it would have happened. I could not understand why it would have happened."

Stutzman said he continued home to Ohio, where he told a number of people different stories about Danny's whereabouts and death.

"I guess I did not want to face the fact that he actually had died. I had difficulty accepting that."

Gallup wrapped it up.

"As you sit there right now, you don't know what caused your son's death, is that a fair statement?"

"Right."

Gallup reminded Stutzman that a Saint Louis pathologist had favored the conclusion that Danny had died a natural death.

"Would that help let you sleep a little better?"

"Yes, I believe so."

It was defense attorney Dan Werner's turn, and though he was glad for the chance to confront the accused, he wished that he'd had more time to prepare. Maybe information would have come to light possibly leading to an investigation that would result in an abuse or murder charge.

"Now," Werner continued, "you just told me that you were in Nebraska and stopped at a large truck stop near Salina, Kansas, to eat, is that right?"

"I do remember Salina, Kansas, the following morning."

"The following morning?"

"Yes, but not while I had my son with me."

"And you stated to him that Danny got out, but didn't eat very much. But you have told me today that Danny ate fairly well at the truck stop. Which is correct?"

Again Stutzman seemed confused, and his voice was nearly inaudible.

"He dished out— what he dished out for himself, he did not eat all of it."

It was about midnight— time for Danny's medication, Stutzman said— when he tried to wake him.

"I reached back, I got a hold of his leg, and he wouldn't wake up. So I pulled over and reached back again and couldn't figure it out. So I got out of the car and went around the back of the car and opened the back end where he had his head back there. And I noticed right way, or shortly, the look on his face—there was something wrong."

"What did you notice about his face?" Werner asked.

"His eyes were, like, rolled back in his head, and his complexion did not look like it normally does."

"What did his complexion look like?"

"White."

"What did you do?"

Stutzman said he tried mouth-to-mouth resuscitation. But Danny remained still, his eyes rolled back.

Werner retraced what had been said in court that morning.

"Mr. Stutzman, when you noticed his eyes rolled back, when you couldn't get a pulse, why did you not seek help for Danny at that time?"

"That's what I keep— still keep asking myself today. I had difficulty believing that it had happened. I could not figure out why it happened. I wish now I would have."

"Could Danny have been alive at that time?"

"I don't think it is possible. Well, I'm not going to swear to it, but I don't think so at all, because at the time there was no pulse and I spent several— at least several more hours with him after that, and he never did breathe during that time."

"This was after you pulled off the road that you spent several hours with him?"

"Yes."

"Were you outside the car when you spent that time with him?"

"I kept him in the car until I left him. But, yes, I did get out of the car some of the time."

"Could Danny have been alive when you placed him in that ditch?"

"I don't see any way possible."

"Do you recall Officer Garber asking you that question down in Azle, Texas, after your arrest?"

"No, I don't."

Werner probed further.

"Do you recall telling Garber when asked, was Danny alive when you put him in the ditch, do you recall telling him, 'That is a good question. I don't think so, but he could have been?' "

"No, I don't recall that."

"Mr. Stutzman, did you kill Danny?"

The room was so quiet that no one had difficulty hearing the man's response.

"No, I did not."

"Did you help Danny die in any way?"

"No."

"Do you remember anything else about Danny's death that you haven't told us about?"

"No, not that I can think of. Only thing I can say, it's real tragic. I still, to this day, don't know why or exactly what—"

"Did— what did you do when you placed him in the ditch?"

Again, Stutzman was very quiet.

"I told him another prayer. I decided to leave him and let God take care of him."

He said he pulled off the road, parked, and carried the boy's limp body to a ditch and covered him with snow. He got back on the main road and headed south.

STUTZMAN PLEADED GUILTY TO TWO MISDEMEANOR charges of unlawful disposal of a dead human body and concealing the death. To the people of Chester, Nebraska, who had loved, cared for, and buried little Danny, it was hardly justice.

The presiding judge sentenced Stutzman to 18 months in jail.

"I really wasn't happy with it, but there's not much you can do," Thayer County Sheriff Gary Young said. Young had been first on the scene after the boy's body was found.

But Stutzman's legal problems were far from over.

After serving his sentence in Nebraska, he was transported to Austin, Texas, where he was put on trial for the death of Glen Pritchett, his former roommate. Pritchett, who had worked for Stutzman's remodeling business, was found in a ditch in May 1985 in southeast Travis County. He'd been shot once in the head.

When he had first been questioned by deputies, Stutzman said he had not seen Pritchett for two months and believed he had returned to Montana to be with family. Soon after, he and his son moved from Austin. Actually, they'd been on the run, and they'd run to Durango, Colorado.

In 1989 Stutzman was convicted of killing Pritchett. While he was serving sixteen years of his forty year sentence he emerged as a key suspect in the Colorado murders of David Tyler and Dennis Slaeter.

Tyler was found dead Nov. 10, 1985, in a small utility trailer outside Automatic Transmission Exchange, a business he co-owned in Durango, Colorado. Slaeter was found shot to death just a few weeks later, on Dec. 5, 1985, in the basement of Junction Creek Liquors, where he worked as a clerk.

Evidence suggests Stutzman and Tyler knew each other and possibly attended the same party two days before Tyler's body was found. Both men were gay and used drugs.

The police found a bloody palm print in the automotive shop where Tyler was killed. The print was kept in an evidence locker at the Durango Police Department, with hopes that one day there would be a match.

Eli Stutzman was released from prison in 2002.

AFTER ELI STUTZMAN WAS PAROLED HE LIVED quietly in the Fort Worth area. He never mentioned Danny to his lovers or friends. In 2007, HIV-positive and fifty-six years old, he killed himself.

After his death a friend tried to contact Eli's relatives. He had known nothing of the crimes they told him about. In fact, he described him as a "kind, soft-spoken friend who loved animals and made and sold leather goods from his home."

Until Eli's death, police had never obtained his DNA and a suitable palm print. Now they could and sent them to Colorado. Although the print didn't match the bloody print left on the wall where David Tyler was murdered, Stutzman remains a suspect.

As for the child known as "little boy blue," the small town with the big heart, Chester, Nebraska, still cares for the gravesite of Danny Stutzman. People still lay toys, cars and coins on his grave. The community built a roadside memorial for him, then rebuilt it after a tornado.

The Son Who Blew Up The Night

The Bombing of United 629, Denver, 1955
By Ron Franscell

ALWAYS THE DUTIFUL SON, JACK GRAHAM LUGGED his mother's heavy luggage to the weighing counter in Denver's Stapleton Municipal Airport, where she would catch her evening flight to Portland, the first stop on an Alaskan adventure.

He waited in line with her, making small talk until they reached the scales. Their life together hadn't always been pleasant, but she counted on him.

There, an airline clerk told Daisie King her bags were 37 pounds too heavy and she'd have to pay an extra fee. Instead, the frugal Daisie asked Jack if she should unpack some of her stuff.

"Mother, I'm sure you will need it," he insisted.

Daisie, who was 53, and Jack, 23 years old, were famous for their spats over the smallest details, so it was surprising when Daisie paid the fee without protest, kissed her son and his family goodbye, and boarded her plane.

Jack treated his wife, 21-year old Gloria, and son to a quick dinner in the airport's coffee shop, but not long after they sat down, Jack started feeling sick. He excused himself from the table briefly and went to the men's room, blaming his sour stomach on bad coffee and the excitement of his mother's departure.

On the way home, unaware that a mechanical glitch had delayed Daisie's takeoff, Jack mentioned to his wife that he'd put a little surprise in his mother's luggage.

At 6:52 p.m. on November 1, 1955, just eleven minutes after take-off, United Air Lines Flight 629, a DC-6B carrying 44 people, exploded in the night sky, raining fire, metal, and body parts on empty sugar-beet fields about 32 miles north of Denver, near Longmont, nearly six thousand feet below.

With one tiny, spectacular spark, Daisie King and everyone else aboard became a part of the night sky forever.

IT SEEMED LIKE ANOTHER TRAGIC ACCIDENT. JUST A month before, another United plane smashed into a mountain in Medicine Bow Peak, Wyoming, killing 66. In fact, United had lost two other airliners on that same route since the end of the war. The corridor was considered so snake-bitten, a United executive told reporters the next day, "Sabotage is not considered."

The crash site was a grisly horror.

That night, small fires illuminated a scene straight out of Hell. Wreckage and mangled corpses of United 629 were strewn for a mile across two family farms six miles east of Longmont. A young priest with a flashlight walked among the scattered, burning wreckage into the night, administering last rites to the mangled corpses. For many years to come, farmers would find silverware, eyeglasses and other grim reminders of the tragedy in the tilled soil.

The next day, stunned federal investigators started literally piecing together the puzzling catastrophe, collecting thousands of fragments of scattered fuselage, luggage, hundreds of pieces of mail, personal items—and grisly pieces of exploded corpses. In an empty hangar at Stapleton airport, they put the shattered plane back together, bit by ghastly bit. No piece was large than an automobile.

The airline's tail section had been cleanly severed, and fell intact a half-mile from the main debris field. The rear-most section of the cargo hold had been shredded with devastating force. Agents could smell gunpowder on everything. Then, on the surfaces of the plane's worst-damaged section, they found sodium carbonate, nitrate, and sulfur—residue from a dynamite blast.

Investigators sifting through the dirt found something more: four pieces of sooty, scarred sheet metal that weren't part of the plane. One of them was red with the blue letters: HO. It was the metal side of a six-volt battery. Was it meaningless debris ... or could it have been the detonator?

Airline sabotage was so rare in 1955—it was suspected in only two air crashes before that, in 1933 and 1949—it didn't feel like the most logical conclusion. But after six days of intensive examination of the evidence, the feds strongly suspected the crash of United 629 had not been an accident.

As the grim task of identifying the bodies in a temporary morgue continued, FBI agents interviewed witnesses, combed the passenger list, and closely examined the luggage and personal effects for clues. Who would blow up an airplane of innocent people? More importantly, why? Had one passenger been the target? Who stood to gain from the tragedy?

The agents were stumped.

One passenger's luggage had been damaged more than the rest. Agents linked it to Daisie King, 54, a successful businesswoman. And scattered around King's remains they found the contents of her purse: some personal letters, a checkbook, $1,000 in traveler's checks, an address book, and two keys for safety deposit boxes—and some newspaper clippings about her 23-year-old son Jack Graham, a convicted forger and troublemaker.

It got worse. Agents discovered Graham had also collected insurance money after a mysterious explosion at his mother's East Denver hamburger stand less than six months before. Plus, he stood to inherit part of his mother's $150,000 estate, and had taken out six flight-insurance policies on his mother the day she died—all naming him as the beneficiary.

Ironically, they were worthless. Daisie King had signed none of them.

Suddenly, the FBI had a person of interest.

Jack Graham hated his mother. His youth was turbulent. He was born to Daisie and her second husband. He had an older sister for Daisie's previous marriage, which ended in divorce. When Graham's father died of pneumonia in 1937, the impoverished, unemployed Daisie left him in an orphanage. She married a wealthy Colorado rancher in 1941, but didn't reunite with Jack until 1954, when her third husband died and left her with a handsome inheritance.

Graham grew up a strange child who couldn't stay out of trouble but often dodged any serious punishment. He'd been convicted of forgery, owning illegal guns, and bootlegging liquor, but by 1954 Daisie thought he might have put his bad days behind him. He married a nice girl and had two children, so she paid his fines, bought him a home in Denver, and gave him a job managing her hamburger joint.

But Jack still nursed a simmering grudge against Daisie. They often quarreled, especially about money. He also was skimming money from the cash register.

In May 1955, a gas explosion gutted the building. Police suspected arson, but no charges were ever filed, so Graham collected $1,200 from the insurance company. Soon after, he bought a new truck that inexplicably stalled on a railroad track and was destroyed by an oncoming train. Again, he collected the insurance money.

Less than two weeks after the plane crash, Jack and Gloria Graham welcomed FBI agents into their home on West Mississippi Avenue in Denver. In a pleasant interview, they described Daisie's red-and-black plaid luggage, but Jack told them he had no idea what his mother had packed in it—she was very picky about such things, he said, and didn't allow him to help her—but he knew she'd taken a lot of shotgun shells and high-powered rifle ammunition because she wanted to hunt caribou in Alaska.

Then Gloria mentioned the "little surprise" Jack told her he'd put in Daisie's bag. Jack had wrapped it secretly in the basement, but she believed it was a tool set.

The same day, a neighbor told agents how Jack Graham had gotten ill and pale after his mother's plane took off. When Jack heard a Denver airliner had crashed that night, she said, his response chilled her.

"That is it," is all he said.

Things didn't add up, and the FBI finally told Jack Graham he was a prime suspect. The cocky Graham said he had nothing to hide, volunteered for a lie-detector test, and permitted agents to search his home, cars and property.

It might have been his biggest mistake.

In the Grahams' house, the FBI found bomb-making parts that matched debris at the crash, as well as the six insurance policies he'd bought at the airport on the day of the crash.

Confronted with the evidence against him, Jack Graham had only one question:

"Where do you want me to start?"

He spilled everything. He admitted the explosion at the hamburger joint, and leaving his new truck to be hit by a train. And he confessed that he'd blown up United 629.

His "little surprise" for his mother was 25 sticks of dynamite, a six-volt battery, and two electric primer caps on a timer set to go off in 60 minutes. He not only hoped to collect money on his mother's travel insurance and from her estate, he wanted to even the score on his old animosities against his mom.

He had rigged the timer to explode over the rugged Rockies, where a search would be difficult, if not impossible. But an unexpected, 35-minute delay in takeoff meant the plane blew up while still ascending just 40 miles north of Denver.

Graham was charged with sabotage, but the maximum penalty on a federal sabotage charge was only 10 years, so he was handed over to state authorities and charged with first-degree murder.

Graham immediately pleaded insanity. Four psychiatrists found him completely sane and he was scheduled for trial.

In jail, he spent his days studiously reading, avoiding trouble. One night, guards found him garroted with his own socks, barely conscious, and he was again admitted in a straitjacket to the psychiatric ward under 24-hour surveillance.

But it proved a turning point in his behavior. He began talking freely to the psychiatrists, to whom he revealed the seeds of his mass murder.

After he'd decided to murder his mother, he bought a timer and some dynamite for his homemade bomb. He built it in his basement while his mother made her final travel preparations. When she wasn't looking, he slipped the brown paper-wrapped box of dynamite into her suitcase and sealed it tight before they left for the airport.

At Stapleton, he let Daisie and his family off at the front door while he parked the car. But before he hauled the suitcase to the terminal, he set the timer.

But looking back at all the destruction, the doctors asked him, how did it make him feel?

"I realized that there were about 50 or 60 people carried on [such an airliner]," he said, "but the number of people to be killed made no difference to me; it could have been a thousand. When their time comes, there is nothing they can do about it."

Graham added that it was a great relief to talk about the mass murder of 44 people, including his mother, because it had been weighing heavily on him.

Although he later recanted his confession, Graham's trial started five and a half months after the crash. It was the hottest ticket in Colorado. Throughout the three-week trial, hundreds of curious court-watchers and reporters waited for hours in the halls outside the courtroom, hoping to get seats. Some brought sack lunches. But only one seat was saved: Every morning, precisely at nine a.m., a young pretty woman took her seat just a few feet behind Jack Graham.

She was the wife of United 629's pilot, Lee H. Hall, 39 years old the night his plane exploded.

Graham had lost weight in jail, but remained unflappable during the trial. Each day, he wore a new suit to court. The FBI noted that he slouched in his chair, chewed gum, and occasionally conferred with his attorneys, always unmoved—even when the district attorney, in his opening statement, said the facts would prove Jack Graham killed Daisie King and 43 other people "coldly, carefully, and deliberately."

Prosecutors called 80 different witnesses, including the shopkeeper who sold Graham the dynamite and blasting, and entered 174 exhibits into evidence; the defense had eight witnesses. Although he'd told reporters he would deliver bombshell evidence of his innocence at the trial, Graham refused to testify on his own behalf.

The jury needed nothing more. After deliberating only 69 minutes, they found Jack Gilbert Graham guilty of first-degree murder and recommended the death penalty.

Awaiting execution, he admitted to a reporter the same pitiless, twisted credo he'd shared with the shrinks.

"As far as feeling any remorse for these people, I don't. I can't help it. Everybody pays their way and takes their chances. That's just the way it goes."

Graham was executed in the gas chamber at the Colorado State Penitentiary on Friday, January 11, 1957, 12 days before his 25th birthday, and was pronounced dead at 8:08 p.m.

The bombing of United 629—then only the second proven case of a deliberate airline bombing over the U.S. mainland—remains the fifth deadliest mass murder in American history. Lessons the FBI learned on United 629 proved valuable for even more complex airline disasters, such as the terrorist bombing of Pan Am 103 over Lockerbie, Scotland, in 1988.

Daisie King's remains were buried under a simple headstone at Denver's Fairmount Cemetery. After her son's execution, his ashes were scattered around her grave.

Confessions of a Bitch on Wheels

IT'S BEEN YEARS SINCE SHARON NELSON HAS indulged in her favorite pastimes. Shopping for low-cut blouses and high-cut skirts. Getting her nails lacquered. Marrying for money. Meeting a lover at a motel. Arranging to have her husband killed.

One of America's most famous black widows—those women who kill their husbands or have someone kill for them, usually in the name of money—Sharon Nelson was raised to be a good girl.

She found it a hell of a lot more exciting to be bad.

The second of three daughters, Sharon Douglas grew up in a strict Seventh-Day Adventist family in Ohio. Seventh-Day Adventism, founded in America in the 1840s, is more than a religion—it is a culture, a way of life. Members believe that the Bible is the literal translation of the word of God. The body is a temple, so Adventists don't smoke, drink alcohol or eat meat. They are modest, don't wear jewelry, tithe ten percent of their income, and believe the second coming of Christ is imminent. Church services are on Saturdays.

Sharon's mother was distant but her father spent a lot of time with her. Along the way, he taught her that the rules could be bent a little. When she went with him to the hardware or feed store, he'd buy her a Coke, although their church forbids caffeine. That didn't shock Sharon, but finding her father's girlie magazines did. "We'd sneak up there and look at them. Our daddy didn't do things like that," her sister Judy said later. It seemed as though their father wanted to live in two worlds: the church's world and the real world.

When Sharon was in grade-school she learned for the first time that despite what they preached, other adults broke the rules to devastating and far-reaching consequences. She was a beautiful little girl then, with gorgeous eyes and thick, curly hair. She was also a target.

Two incidents took place before she was ten.

Sharon had no reason to feel anything but safe sitting in the backseat of the car while a group of Seventh-Day Adventists went out to raise money for the support of the church. As they went from house to house, eight-year-old Sharon sat sandwiched between two men. One of the men put his hand on her lap.

"I'm tired," the church member said. "And my hands are very cold."

Sharon felt his fingers slide up under her skirt and pull at her panties. She pulled her legs tighter together. She yanked at his arm, but said nothing.

A couple of years later, it happened again. This time, the abuser was an elderly janitor at the church school. Sharon had heard stories from other girls that the man's hands wandered, but she thought she was safe because she was good friends with his family. She was wrong. One afternoon when she went to get some cleaning supplies from the storage closet, the old man pushed her inside and grabbed her crotch and fondled her.

She told her mother, but years later her mother had no memory of the incident.

Sharon seemed to start her adult life on the right path. In 1963, when she was eighteen, she married an Adventist minister, Mike Fuller. But soon she was taking time away from typing up her husband's sermons to having sex with men in the church. Lots of sex. Five years later, she had two children, only one fathered by her husband.

Mike changed churches in an effort to put some miles between Sharon and her boyfriends. His jobs took the family to North Carolina, and then to Trinidad, Colorado, a former mining town just 20 miles north of New Mexico. The town has an unusual moniker—the "sex change capitol of the world." It earned the name after Dr. Stanley Biber, a local surgeon, began performing sex reassignment surgery in the 1960s.

Sharon and Mike were welcomed by the members of their new Adventist congregation—but quickly the women became wary of the new minister's wife. The lusty lady made an immediate impression on their husbands. A dark pageboy framed her pretty face. She had full cheeks and fuller lips. She liked to be called "Sher." When she wore short-shorts, skipped the bra, undid a few buttons on her blouse, and winked at men in church, they were goners.

Sharon became the talk of the church and the town because she had taken up coffee, alcohol, smoking, sunbathing in the nude and coveting her neighbor's husband. She was breaking the Ten Commandments right and left.

"Lock up your husbands! Sharon's here!" one woman told her friends whenever she saw Sharon approaching her front door.

As someone once said, Sharon gave trash a bad name.

JULIE NELSON DIDN'T LOCK UP HER HUSBAND QUICK enough. Perry Nelson was forty-three years old, an optometrist, well-off, the owner of a small plane, and the married father of three when he met Sharon and Mike Fuller.

Soon, Sharon was working for Perry in his office. Their affair was a badly-kept secret. His office manager and close friend, Barb Ruscetti, knew there was a lot more than eye exams going on in the back office. For convenience, Perry parked his motorhome nearby so the two of them could take their breaks on a mattress. It was Barb that coined the term "bitch on wheels" for Sharon. They were found out and their spouses confronted them at a motel.

Mike had had it. He had forgiven Sharon's indiscretions for years. He divorced Sharon and took the children.

Sharon and Perry married. She showed her affection for her step-children by buying them alcohol. She had two more children. And then what always happened to Sharon happened again. She grew bored.

At a costume party she met Gary Starr Adams, who was married and the father of a grown daughter and a young son. Sharon was dressed as the flirty Scarlett O'Hara. Gary was dressed as a mountain man.

Soon, they were meeting in private. She bedded him, over and over. He was a carpenter and would never have been able to give her the home and lifestyle she was used to, but she loved frolicking with him and said he might have been the only man she ever loved.

She and Perry were fighting over money problems. They had bought land and were building a new house in Rocky Ford they called the Round House because the house had high ceilings and featured a six-sided great room. That was tapping them out, plus Perry had his ex-wife and children to support. Sharon wanted Perry to declare bankruptcy but he refused.

She and Perry separated and were contemplating divorce when Sharon struck again—she took up with Buzz Reynolds, a rancher and one of Perry's best friends. When she became pregnant by Buzz, he threw her out so Sharon did what she had done at least five times over the years—she had an abortion. Perry was shocked and ashamed that Sharon and his best friend were having an affair, but he paid for the abortion. He tried to explain to his daughter Lorri that despite everything, he still loved Sharon.

And then Sharon Douglas Fuller Nelson had an idea. The travel trailer wasn't rocking much anymore, and Perry was broke. How could she be free of him yet come away with some money? He just happened to have a $200,000 life insurance policy.

In Gregg's book about Sharon Nelson, *Bitch on Wheels* (first published as *Confessions of An American Black Widow)* he wrote about how Gary Starr Adams bungled the murder of his lover's husband, but kept trying until he finally got it right:

GARY ADAMS WAS NOT ALONE THAT BALMY JUNE night in 1983. He and another man, a friend from way back, waited at the rest stop on 1-25, just outside of Castle Rock. The two smoked cigarettes down to their fibery filters as they passed the time in the cab of Gary's Datsun pickup talking about Sharon and how she had been beaten and abused and ignored by her doctor husband.

Perry didn't love her.
Perry didn't treat her right.

Perry was a mean old bastard.

When a familiar little black VW putted by, Gary and his buddy laid a patch of smoldering rubber to catch up. Perry smiled and laughed out loud when Gary pulled his truck alongside and waved him to follow. They pulled over at a tavern in Castle Rock for a few beers. Gary introduced his friend and told Perry he was heading up to Denver, too.

"Sure was a coincidence that we'd meet on the way up," Gary said.

After downing a few rounds, the three men decided to go to a strip club on the outskirts of Denver. By then, Gary's plan had fully fermented. It was simple and sweet. While he and Perry were in the bathroom, Gary instructed his pal to slip some knockout drops in the doctor's beer. They'd walk the doc out of the place and finish him off.

It was a simple, a good plan. It was a plan all for Sharon.

Back at the table, Perry put the glass to his lips and drank.

After a couple of gulps, he smacked the glass down. He looked disgusted.

"That doesn't taste good at all," he said."Real flat tasting."

Gary said his beer tasted just fine, but Perry didn't want any more.

Perry Nelson held his liquor that night. He didn't get sloppy. He didn't make it easy for Gary to do what he had come there to do. The music blared and the mix of over-the-hill dancers with makeup-covered stretch marks and younger strippers who were working for enough money for implants slid across the stage. As the hours grew later, eyelids became heavy and it was time to go.

"Where do you want to stay?" Perry called out over the club's obnoxiously loud sound system.

Gary had no idea. He had no preference. Neither did his buddy.

"Why don't we just pull over to the side of the road?" he suggested.

With what they all had spent drinking, saving a few bucks on a motel seemed like a good idea. Neither Gary nor his friend knew the doctor had about as much money as they had. Sharon had been reupholstering the VW so he could sleep in it to save on a motel, anyway.

"Perry," Gary said, "don't tell Nancy you saw me up here. I don't want her to know I went to a strip joint."

Perry laughed.

"Don't you tell Sharon, either."

"Promise."

The water of Clear Creek ran through the chasm with the rushing sound that lulls weary travelers to sleep when nightfall comes and they cannot drive a mile further. It was after 2:00 A.M. and the sky was pockmarked with stars poking through pinholes in the blackness when the two vehicles pulled over along the highway in Jefferson County. They were just outside of Golden, west of Denver. Perry popped his seat back and stretched out in the VW, while Gary and his buddy tried to get comfortable in the cramped cab of the pickup.

Even though Perry had let him down by holding his booze with impressive fortitude, Gary Adams still wanted to do the job. But he was tired. His friend was beat. The idea of hitting Perry Nelson over the head with a tire iron sounded like too much work.

"To hell with it," he said to his co-conspirator. "Let's just let it go."

The next morning the three ate breakfast at a Golden cafe, chatted as if they were the best of friends, and waved good-bye.

Gary scratched his head years after, wondering why it was that the plan didn't work that night. It would have been just perfect.

Damn it anyway, he thought.

Hours later in the quiet solitude of Round House, Sharon got the shock of her life: Her husband came home. He was supposed to be dead. She was stunned and mad.

Gary Adams recalled what happened:

"Sharon was positive that Perry was not coming back. So when Perry came back she turned white as a ghost. She wasn't expecting it. She had it in her mind how she was going to tell the cops. How she was going to be the grieving widow. She said she was shaking, turned white as a sheet, you know, scared."

And very disappointed.

Thursday, a week after the fiasco with the dud knockout drops, Gary left Denver in his rearview mirror and returned to Wet Canyon. He had heard he could scrounge up some construction work in Trinidad, though that was not the real reason he came back. He had to see the woman he had disappointed. But before he made his way to Dr. Nelson's office on Country Club Drive, he ran into Sharon and a car salesman in downtown Trinidad.

"What happened?" She whispered her hot breath into his ear. "What happened?"

It was neither the right time nor the right place to talk. Sharon told Gary they'd have to meet another time.

"Perry's in town today," she said. What she meant: Do not come to the office. Do not.

"Maybe we could meet next week?" she said softly, out of earshot of the car salesman. "At the lake."

Trinidad Lake was still one of the lovers' special places. It always would be. Like an incredible sapphire, the lake shimmered across its surface from one side to the other. Conifers met the water like the jagged edge of a two-man saw. Eagles soared overhead searching for the fish that brought sportsmen from all over the region. Trinidad Lake was serene and lovely. Yet within the beauty of it all was a woman mad at the world. Mad at her lover.

Sharon had become increasingly upset in the days after Perry's miraculous return from the dead. She blamed Gary for botching the plan to murder the man who was the source of all her problems. Gary had no idea how hard it had been on her when Perry returned unscathed. Why hadn't he thought of how she would react? It scared her to death. Was he so selfish that could not have warned her that he had failed? Gary hadn't thought of her.

Gary held Sharon, trying to placate her and stop her tirade. He said he would do it again, but not right away. He suggested they might have to wait awhile, perhaps another year.

Sharon's face froze in disbelief. She wouldn't hear of it.

"Oh no, no," she said. "Perry's got another meeting up in Denver in July. It would be better to do it then."

Though Gary had hoped they'd have sex that afternoon, they didn't. Sharon said she was too upset.

A few days after the lake rendezvous, Sharon invited Gary and Nancy Adams to join her and Perry for dinner up at Round House. Though the timing was suspect, the invitation was not unusual. The Adamses and the Nelsons occasionally got together to play cards, share a dinner or drink coffee or beer. Despite what she had done with Nancy's husband, Sharon still considered the quiet, gentle woman her friend. After the meal, while the women stayed in the kitchen talking, Gary and Perry visited outside on the driveway. Gary told Perry he had heard he was heading back to Denver and he wondered if he could catch a ride.

"I'm going up there to buy some mini-14s," Gary said, piquing Perry's interest. The guns were stolen and selling for about $50, a bargain. Several men in the canyon had mini-14s and considered the combat-quality firearm perfect for shooting coyotes, even deer. Perry definitely wanted one.

Gary's voice took on a conspiratorial tone. "Don't tell Nancy," he said. "She doesn't know I'm going to go up there for that. She thinks I'm going to go up there to make some money."

Perry laughed. He wouldn't tell her anything.

A week later, Gary Adams was working at a Trinidad construction site when he got word to Nancy that he wouldn't be coining home that Thursday night. He was going to stay in town to play poker with his buddies. He parked his Datsun at a repair center, telling the mechanics that his brakes needed work.

Next, he called the eye clinic on Country Club Drive.

Sharon, of course, answered.

"I'm planning on catching a ride with Perry," Gary said.

"Fine," she said as she handed the phone to her husband.

"On your way out," Gary said, "can you stop by and pick me up and we'll go up there and get the guns?"

Perry thought it was a fine idea.

The drive from Trinidad to Denver is a long one. Four hours, six hours—depending on how fast one drives and how many pit stops are needed along the way. It is a beautiful drive up 1-25 nonetheless: mountains rising to the west and the last edge of the Great Plains to the east. As the black VW sped along, Gary mostly listened as Perry chatted on about his life, his children and, of course, Sharon.

Sharon, he said, had purchased some emeralds from the back pages of a magazine.

"Some investment," Perry said shaking his head with a disgusted laugh. "Turns out when she went to sell them that they are worthless."

An animated Perry carried the bulk of the conversation as he pressed his foot against the floorboard and zipped down the highway. The doc was a genuinely nice guy, Gary thought. He didn't have a bad word for anyone. Gary was no expert on human behavior, but as far as he could tell it seemed out of character that Perry Nelson was an abuser of his wife and children. The bruises Sharon had pointed out on her body began to gnaw at the VW's passenger. Gary Adams wondered if he had been duped. While smacking Sharon wasn't out of the realm of possibilities, considering how she acted some of the time, Dr. Nelson didn't seem the type to do it.

"I don't think I'll ever see my older girls again," Perry said at one point on the drive. His words were full of resignation and Gary chose not to follow up on the comment. He didn't know if it was because of a wedge Sharon had driven between the girls and their father, though, he figured, that could have been the reason for it. Sharon had complained about the grown daughters.

Gary changed the subject. With what was on his mind, the comment bothered him.

It was close to 7:00 P.M. when the city of Pueblo came into view and they stopped for a bite at the Burger King. Perry had a chicken sandwich and Gary ate a hamburger. After eating, they zipped over to the mall so Perry could say hello to a friend who ran a Pearle Vision optical center there. When they pulled up it was obvious they were too late. The mall had closed.

Though Perry was disappointed, Gary felt relieved. He didn't want to see anyone; he didn't want anyone to see him.

Nothing really stops a Colorado highway. Mountains that get in the way are bored clear through. Ledges are blasted out of granite slopes and roads are laid in like Band-Aids. A mile above tunnel one on Highway 6, near Golden, is Clear Creek. In the summer it is a scenic spot for a picnic as water gently runs the rocky gauntlet. Boulders rise high enough from the water for kids to hopscotch across one side to an-other. But spring and fall bring a different picture. Water courses through a rocky canyon making Clear Creek neither clear nor a creek.

A diamond-shaped road sign warned travelers who pulled over to rest or take photographs: CLIMB TO SAFETY IN CASE OF FLASH FLOOD.

Though it had been raining intermittently for hours, the clouds opened up and the freeway became the world's largest car wash. By the time the VW reached the creek, it was a full-fledged downpour. As they went through the tunnel, Gary asked Perry to pull over.

"Got to take a piss," the younger man said.

As Gary walked back to the car he told Perry he had lost his wallet. Perry offered to help him look and walked into the woods for the last time. Gary hit him plenty hard and dragged him into the lake. Perry struggled far longer than Gary had thought he could. In fact, forensics experts said the frigid water might have helped Perry's fight for survival.

It was around 4:00 A.M. when Gary made it back to his place in the canyon. His blue jeans had dried by then, but his muscular body still hurt like hell. He winced vaguely as he pulled into the dusty driveway leading to the Dude Ranch. He was wired and agitated. He told himself Perry was dead, but he couldn't be sure of it. He hoped that he was dead, because if he wasn't there would be hell to pay. If Perry was alive, Gary knew he was going to jail for a long, long time. He watched the sun rise and paced the floor.

At 9:00 A.M., Gary could take just sitting around no more. He had to do something. He announced to his wife, Nancy that he needed to take care of some business in Ratone, about an hour away. On the way out the door, he suggested a quick detour.

"Perry owes me some money," he said to Nancy as she got into the car. "Let's go by there and see if he's home."

Nancy agreed. Since it was early, she'd sit in the car while Gary ran inside to get the cash. It wasn't polite to go bother neighbors without a phone call or an invitation.

Sharon answered the door in her bathrobe, slit open to reveal most of her ample breasts.

"Everything is okay," he said. "Perry's not coming back." He didn't tell her he was not absolutely positive about it, because he worried that she'd get more skittish than he already was.

"You're sure?" she asked. "Everything's all right?"

"Everything's okay."

Sharon fished around for a hundred dollars and handed the money to her mountain man.

"You're sure he's not coming back?" she asked once more.

"No, he's not."

Gary and Nancy Adams spent the day and night in a Raton motel, a good hour from what Gary had assumed would be the heat of a crime investigation. Nancy, of course, had no idea why they needed to get away. She was just glad to be alone with her husband. When they made love, Nancy never noticed the scrapes and bruises on her husband's body. At least, she never said anything about it.

Nancy, Gary believed, suspected nothing. And why would she? Gary was certain his wife liked Sharon. Friends don't steal another friend's husband.

"Sharon and Nancy were best friends," he said later. "It might sound crazy, but I had everything covered."

everyone thought Sharon and Gary had murdered Perry, but there was no proof. Perry Nelson's body wasn't found for thirteen months. When it was, his death was ruled an accident and Sharon collected the $200,000 in life insurance plus another $50,000 in death benefits.

She didn't forget to show Gary that she was grateful. She bought him a new truck, gave him $10,000 cash, and put his name on a $5,000 certificate of deposit. She wanted Gary to divorce his wife and marry her, but he stalled. So she bought herself a mink coat and continued to sleep with him while she was on the lookout for a new husband.

Never one to be alone for long, Sharon met and married Glen Harrelson, a firefighter. He was handsome and rugged. Glen was a member of the fire department of Thornton, Colorado, a suburb just north of Denver. It only took less than one year of marriage before Sharon was spending more money than Glen earned. They began to argue and she began to lose interest.

As several men had learned before, when Sharon Douglas Fuller Nelson Harrelson became bored or needed money—watch out.

On November 19, 1988, members of the Thornton fire department were called to a fire at a house at Columbine Court. It was the home of one of their own, forty-five year old Glen Harrelson. He seemed to have been alone in the house when it caught fire. During the first hours of the investigation police made a startling discovery—they found shell casings in the burned out house.

After they retrieved Glen's body, they determined what had happened. He had been ambushed. A killer was lying in wait when Glen entered his house. It was probably over quickly. The intruder shot Glen in the head, doused gasoline on his body, stoked the fire with some clothing, deliberately spilled a jar of coins, and left. It was a classic case of a staged homicide, and it only took the killer a few minutes to do it.

SHARON FINALLY CONFESSED AT HER FAVORITE Pizza Hut.

Detectives Glen Trainor and Elaine Tygart of the Thornton, Colorado police department had met with Sharon before about the murder of her husband Glen Harrelson. It was tricky trying to put together an accurate picture of her marriages, love affairs, and dead husbands.

When they asked to meet with her again, she suggested the Pizza Hut in Walsenburg, about two hours from Denver. So they drove her and her young children from her marriage to Perry Nelson, Danny and Misty, to the restaurant. As they slid into the Naugahyde booth they gave the children a fistful of quarters to play arcade games in front of the restaurant.

This was a place of memories for Sharon. She and Gary had eaten at the Pizza Hut. She'd brought her children there. She had even been caught once trying to sneak out without paying the bill. It was where Perry had broken down and cried uncontrollably as he told his wife, Julie, that he couldn't give up Sharon.

Tygart and Trainor had a hunch she was going to tell them who had killed Glen Harrelson.

She told them that and so much more.

"I'm tired of living a lie," she said.

Advised of her rights and after signing a waiver, she began. "It all began a long time ago," she said, as if narrating a bedtime story.

It wasn't the story of a naïve princess. It was the tale of a monster.

Police later described her confession as matter-of-fact and unemotional. She showed no remorse. They said she confessed because she knew she wouldn't be able to get away with a second murder, and planned to blame it all on Gary.

She tried to. She metaphorically pointed a long, red, fingernail at Gary Adams and accused him of killing for love and money—her love and her money.

THE THORNTON POLICE CALLED SHARON NELSON "extremely narcissistic, cold and calculating, a manipulator."

Gregg Olsen corresponded with Sharon after she and Gary Adams were sentenced for the murders of Perry Nelson and Glen Harrelson. During an episode about Sharon on *Investigation Discovery's Deadly Women,* he described her as, "an oversexed, bed-hopping, trashy person, who thought she was the belle of the ball."

Sharon pleaded guilty to two counts of first-degree murder, telling the world she had forfeited her right to a pair of murder trials to spare her children. Others speculated that she feared the death penalty. Gary Adams held out longer than his lover, insisting through his attorney that he was not guilty of anything.

But in the end, he also pleaded guilty to two counts of first-degree murder when he was told that the love-of-his-life would testify against him. He also made one last mistake concerning the whereabouts of the gun used to kill Glen Harrelson. Gary told a jailhouse snitch where he had hidden it. Authorities found it under his porch steps.

When Sharon Nelson is heard from—which isn't often these days—she maintains her innocence. She says her confession was a big mistake and that she was manipulated by authorities. She was a battered woman who had feared for her life. She is a victim.

Gary says he still loves Sharon. He concedes that he killed Glen Harrelson but he remains less forthcoming about his exact role in the murder of Perry Nelson. Yes, he tried to drown Perry that night in Clear Creek and smashed his head with a rock.

"But he was alive, when I saw him last. He was alive," he said.

The surviving Nelson children—including Misty and Danny—filed a claim against the insurance companies that paid off Sharon, the killer of their father. The insurance investigators had always been suspicious of Sharon but had never told the police that she had purchased five of her six life insurance policies within a week of Perry's murder or that she had sold off his belongings and assets within days of his disappearance.

Some wonder if the insurance companies had been more forthcoming with the authorities, Sharon and Gary might have been prosecuted years before and Glen Harrelson's life might have been saved.

Sharon is serving her sentence at the La Vista Correctional Facility in Pueblo, Colorado. Gary Adams is housed at Colorado's Limon Correctional Facility.

Who knows, maybe they'll still get a chance to be together someday. It would be a late-in-life marriage. They'll both be in their eighties before they're eligible for parole.

PHOTO ARCHIVE

Mountains of Tragedy Photos

Critics felt that JonBenet was inappropriately "sexed up" for the beauty pageants she entered.

The Ramsey home in Boulder, Colorado where 6-year old JonBenet was found murdered in the basement Dec. 26, 1996.

From the beginning, suspicion fell on John and Patsy Ramsey. They gave few interviews before one with ABC's Barbara Walters in 2000.

Eric Harris Dylan Klebold

Eric Harris and Dylan Klebold in yearbook photos.

Harris and Klebold shown on surveillance video as passed through the cafeteria.

On July 20, 2012, James Holmes entered an Aurora movie theater and allegedly killed shot and killed 12 people and injured 70 others.

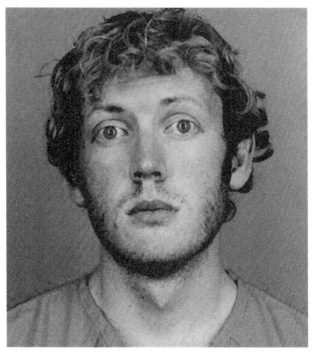

Holmes, with dyed orange hair, is in jail, awaiting trial.

Her Lover's Wife Photos

Brian Hood

Jennifer Reali couldn't resist Brian Hood's good looks—or killing for him.

The Amish Serial Killer Photos

Eli Stutzman was gay, a serial killer—and Amish.

After his pregnant wife Ida died in a mysterious barn fire, Eli dragged his son Daniel with him across the country.

Eli left Daniel's body in a ditch. The town of Chester, Nebraska named the unknown child Matthew and buried him. His identity wasn't discovered for two years.

The Son Who Blew Up the Night Photos

Daisie King had many ups and downs in her relationship with her son, Jack Graham. She didn't know his anger and greed would turn to murder.

Jack Graham killed 44 people in his quest to benefit from life insurance policies he bought on his mother.

Confessions of a Bitch on Wheels Photos

Sharon Nelson was raised to be a good girl and married a minister. She quickly became very bad.

Gary Adams would do almost anything for Sharon—even kill for her.

THE DEADLY DAUGHTER-IN-LAW

GREGG OLSEN
AND
REBECCA MORRIS

Notorious
Arizona

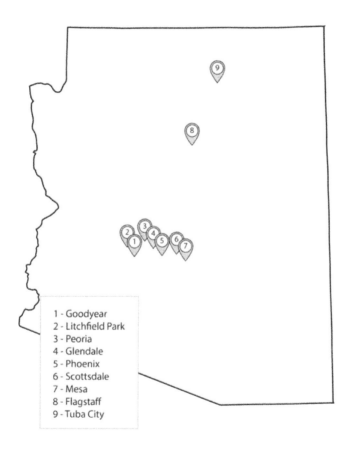

1 - Goodyear
2 - Litchfield Park
3 - Peoria
4 - Glendale
5 - Phoenix
6 - Scottsdale
7 - Mesa
8 - Flagstaff
9 - Tuba City

The Fourth Wife

NO MORE WOMEN CAN FALL IN LOVE WITH WILLIAM Delaney. Too many of those who did, died or disappeared.

Police in Peoria, Arizona are still trying to discover exactly what happened to wife number three, Jayme Delaney, and number four, Deborah Delaney.

The man with the secrets is dead. But maybe, just maybe, the deaths of two women can still be solved. Jayme and Deborah deserve that.

Peoria, Arizona has it all—trails in the foothills for hiking and biking, the rugged beauty of the desert, baseball spring training for *two* major league teams, and recreation on the Salt River and Lake Pleasant.

A major suburb of Phoenix, Money magazine named Peoria one of America's "Top 100 Places to Live."

Some visitors are drawn by the area's history of gold mines. Armed with a metal detector, hikers search the desert northwest of Peoria on their own—or pay one of a number of companies a fee to experience the full gold mining vacation, complete with a guide, metal detectors, picks, a dry washer, and advice about avoiding rattlesnakes.

On February 6, 2013, two hikers prospecting for gold in the desert near State Route 74, also known as Carefree Highway, stumbled onto something, but it wasn't gold—it was skeletal remains. They guessed that the bones were human and they were right. A female skull, pelvis and ribs were scattered in the dust.

When detectives from the Peoria Police Department rushed to the site, they had one particular cold case in mind they wanted desperately to solve.

SHE HAD ALWAYS LIKED FIREFIGTERS. LOTS OF women do. The muscles. The often rugged good looks. The bravery. According to family, she had been drawn to firefighters since she was 18.

In 2001, Deborah Smyth was 44 years old, a pretty, slender woman with short brown hair and big brown eyes. Early in the year she was trying to meet men on-line. When one wrote her that he had been a firefighter paramedic for years, she was excited.

He told her about himself, at least what he determined was important. He was 45 years old. He was physically fit. He wasn't bad looking. He wore his hair short—departmental regulations.

Eventually, Bill Delaney told Debbie the sad story of his late wife Jayme, who had suffered from multiple sclerosis. He said she had committed suicide by sitting in her vehicle in the garage with the vehicle running and the door closed. The story must have touched Debbie.

Debbie missed the first red flag—Bill Delaney had been on-line looking for romance just seven days after Jayme died. He said nothing about his *other* two marriages.

Debbie and Bill married in 2002. Not much is known about the next several years in their lives. Neighbors said she didn't go out of the house much, except to go to the malls. At some point she was diagnosed and had a name to put to the aches and pains she had felt for years—fibromyalgia. After a hard-won lawsuit, she began receiving social security disability benefits because of the disease.

Later, when he began to threaten Debbie, Bill said that he had worked for the Chicago Police Department and knew people that could "take care of things for him." In truth, he had been a jail paramedic for the sheriff's office in DuPage County, west of Chicago.

Bill retired from the Sun City Fire Department in 2008 and worked for a couple of years for the Montezuma-Rimrock Fire Department until he had a stroke on New Year's Eve of 2010. With physical therapy, he bounced back. He had an okay career, but moved around a bit. Both agencies attributed that to his not being well-liked by his peers. His second wife, Kathryn, had been a nurse for the Department of Corrections and had extensive training in psychology. She said she believed he suffered from a personality disorder and described him this way: "Ego-centric, narcissistic and the center of the universe. It was Bill's way or no way. There are serial killers that people liked better than Bill Delaney."

Debbie was close to her daughter, Soraya Ghiassi, who lived in Iran, and her mother, Patricia Smyth. Soraya said that Bill had always been friendly to her, and treated her like a daughter.

Debbie and Soraya spoke nearly every week by telephone. Debbie didn't tell her daughter or mother much about any marital problems she and Bill may have had. Debbie *did* tell Soraya that he went to on-line porn websites and that he told her openly that he wanted to hook up with couples and liked "kinky" sex involving urine.

The last time Debbie and Soraya spoke by phone, Monday, April 18, 2011, Debbie promised to call on

Easter. Six days later, Easter Sunday, Soraya waited, but her mother didn't call. Soraya discovered that her mother's cell phone had been disconnected. She attempted to e-mail her and she didn't get an answer.

Soraya told her grandmother that she couldn't reach Debbie. The next day, April 26, Debbie's mother, Patricia Smyth, reported her to the police as missing.

When detectives contacted Bill Delaney, he claimed that his wife had left him. He said that when he had left home for a physical therapy appointment on Friday, April 15, 2011, driving their only car, Debbie was alone at the house. When he returned two hours later, she and all of her belongings were gone.

He said he found a note saying Debbie had left with her secret lover, who was wealthy and would provide for her.

He did not report her missing.

Police wondered how a woman in severe pain from fibromyalgia could pack up her belongings and leave in less than two hours—and why she would go to the bother, if she was sneaking away with a rich lover.

The note was odd. It had been typed on a computer—which was missing from the house—had been printed out, and was unsigned.

> *"You don't clean the house right; you don't do anything right, you don't cook for me, you don't bring me my morning coffee, shit I have to bring you coffee you can't even fuck me the way I need to be fucked. You want me to clan and cook? No fuckin way. I had to give up a lot, shopping, road trips, and massages. You lost your job and your money. I need a lot of it and you don't have it anymore you don't pamper me or treat me like the queen that I am. I met a new guy who has a new big house and is going to buy me a new SUV, he*

knows I'm a queen and it's all about me. You and the kids are in the same boat as my birth mother, you are ALL out my life for good. Good luck you'll need it."

Police and Debbie's mother thought there was something fishy about the letter. Patricia Smyth had believed for some time that her daughter was in an abusive relationship. When Debbie had been ill in 2008, her mother thought she had been poisoned. Now she showed the police another letter. Dated February 10, 2007, Debbie had handwritten it, and had her mother read it and witness it at the time.

It read:

"I Deborah Lee Delaney being of sound mind and body do hereby wish to write information in case of my sudden death. I am in fear of my life from my husband (William Raymond Delaney). One reason being I told him I was going to tell the Social Security Admin that he committed fraud by forging his mother's Marnie F. Willie SS# 341-10-1270 DOB 01-31-1915 social security check by signing her SS checks over to himself then signing his name and depositing the SS checks into his AZ Federal Credit Union checking account. I met William on Jan 12, 2001 and checks were deposited until May 2006 to my knowledge. (Williams' mother had been deceased since about 2000.)

"The second reason being, I was told on February 7, 2007 that (by my husband) he was addicted to the 'dark side.' Bondage, spanking, having me pee in his mouth and humiliating him, dressing in women's lingerie and having me fuck him in the ass. We did these things since the early start of our relationship and on and off ending each

time because I did not want to do them anymore because I did not feel comfortable."

Smyth—and the police—noticed the differences in the two letters. The handwritten one had better grammar, good spelling and showed that Debbie was afraid for her life. She had threatened to tell authorities that Bill was forging his deceased mother's social security checks. He told her he'd kill her if she did.

Police decided the author of the typed letter was Bill Delaney.

POLICE PAINSTAKINGLY TRIED TO TRACK DEBBIE'S last days.

In March, about one month before she disappeared, Bill—and maybe Debbie—had signed a deed giving him authority to sell their house without her permission or signature.

In the next few weeks, the couple seemed to take care of routine matters. Only later did some of them seem suspicious.

On April 7, Debbie signed a check to pay for their income tax preparation. On the 11th, she picked up her medical prescriptions as usual. It may have been the last time she was seen. Around that time Bill sold their white Dodge pickup truck, leaving them with one vehicle, a 2001 Jeep Cherokee.

On April 21, Bill had Debbie's cell phone service terminated.

On April 23, Bill asked two firefighters to come to his house early in the morning and help load a heavy footlocker into his Jeep. He told them he was returning fire equipment to Tucson. But he was never employed by Tucson Fire Department and the departments he had worked for—Montezuma-Rimrock and Sun City Fire Departments—couldn't explain why he would return fire equipment to Tucson.

Two days after the heavy footlocker was loaded into Bill's vehicle, Debbie was reported missing. By her mother.

While Bill never bothered to notify the police his wife was missing—she had, after all, chosen to leave, he said—he went out of his way to tell everyone he met, including the firemen, the pharmacist, the family doctor, a realtor, the dentist, neighbors, and anyone else who would listen that she had left him for another man.

If Debbie had chosen to leave her marriage, she left important things undone. She never sent Social Security a new address so she could collect the disability checks she had worked so hard to receive. She didn't take any money out of her checking account with her. Most tellingly, she didn't say anything to her mother or her daughter.

Bill spun a story intended to indict his wife and win sympathy for him. He told people that he had encouraged his wife to find a "sex buddy," since prostate surgery had left him unable to have sex with his wife.

On his Facebook page, Bill wrote: "I work hard, play hard, and love life and the outdoors even more, had a stroke New Year's Eve 2010, wife left me in 4-11."

By June, Bill had moved out of the house and listed it for sale. He packed up his fifth wheeler and drove away, finally settling into a spot at Mormon Lake near Flagstaff.

Soon, Bill Delaney's house of cards would collapse. He told police he had been a SWAT medic—he wasn't. He never had prostate cancer—he had an enlarged prostate, not uncommon, that was treated medically. He waffled on the date he said Deborah had left him.

BILL DELANEY WORKED FAST. BY JUNE HE WAS IN A relationship with a new woman, Judy Vernon. She was 49 years old, a blonde with blue eyes, the mother of two sons, originally from Kansas and Missouri. She was a registered nurse who traveled, essentially free-lancing at a hospital for several months or longer, then moving on to a different assignment.

She met Bill Delaney in a lawyer's office. She was going through a divorce, and Bill was there seeking legal advice for a workers' compensation case. They struck up a conversation in the lobby of the office.

She was living in a mobile home near a medical center in Tuba City, a small community in the Painted Desert on the edge of the Navajo Nation. Her housing was provided by the hospital. Bill Delaney moved his fifth wheeler into her mobile home park. Within a few months, he was living with her.

The Peoria Police Department was convinced that Bill Delaney was responsible for the disappearance—and most likely the murder—of Debbie.

And they were concerned about the health and welfare of the woman who seemed poised to be wife number five, Judy Vernon.

They stepped up surveillance of Bill. As they did, they learned more about his other marriages. They spoke with his second wife, Kathryn, the nurse who had been married to him for ten years. She said it wasn't until the couple tried to buy a home that she found out he had been married before—and still was, to a woman named Nancy. Nancy and Kathryn sometimes spoke on the phone because Nancy had multiple sclerosis and Kathryn could discuss the illness with her. When Kathryn learned that Bill's third wife, Jayme, also had M.S., she was stunned. It seemed that Bill Delaney was attracted to women with debilitating illnesses—and to nurses.

In April, 2012, exactly one year after Debbie disappeared, police had a private talk with Judy Vernon. They had seen her moving things out of her mobile home. She told police that she and Bill were moving to her family home in Missouri. They planned to leave Tuba City in early May.

A detective wrote up his notes after his conversation with Judy Vernon:

> *I asked Vernon if Delaney had told her about any other marriages he had. She said he did not. I then told Vernon that one of the reasons I was talking to her was that I was concerned for her. I told her that I believed that some of the information that Delaney may have shared with her was not true.*
>
> *Vernon looked at me and said, "Like what?"*
>
> *I told Vernon that the wife that committed suicide was not Delaney's first wife, it was his third, and Deborah was his fourth wife. Vernon looked at me and said "Really?"*
>
> *I then asked Vernon what Delaney had told her about his past; with regards to employment, and some of his experiences.*
>
> *Vernon said Delaney had told her that he had been in the military and had been a firefighter.*
>
> *I asked Vernon what Delaney had told her about his assignment while in the military. Vernon said Delaney told her he had been in "Special Operations."*

I advised Vernon that one of things we do as Investigators is to conduct a complete background into all persons involved in an investigation.

I then told Vernon that through our investigation, we had determined that Delaney had never been a member of any of the armed forces.

I told Vernon that it appeared that Delaney had told her two substantial lies with regards to his life experiences. She agreed.

I told Vernon that I was very interested in finding out anything Delaney might have told her with regards to Deborah's disappearance.

Vernon said Delaney had told her that Deborah had left a note when she left. I asked Vernon if Delaney had every shown her the note, and she said he had not.

I asked her what she and Delaney thought or discussed after they discovered that Police had been to the storage locker the week prior. Vernon said she was concerned the Police had ransacked the storage locker. Vernon said Delaney told her, "They are looking for her body." (Meaning Deborah).

I explained to Vernon that we searched the storage locker after a judge had issued a search warrant and told her that search warrants are not issued for no reason, and that probable cause must exist for their issuance. Vernon said she understood.

I then advised Vernon that the main reason we were in Tuba City was to serve additional search warrants on her mobile home, and Delaney's truck and fifth wheel trailer.

I told Vernon that I was concerned with her welfare, and that we had significant issues with the disappearance of Deborah.

Vernon said that the information I had told her definitely "raised some flags."

Vernon asked me what the status of Delaney's former wives. I told her that Delaney's third wife was deceased. I further told her that Delaney's first wife and second wife were still alive and they had been talked to.

I then asked Vernon if Delaney had ever told her he had been a Law Enforcement Officer. She said that Delaney had told her he had been a Police Officer for three years.

I again told her that this was not the case.

I then asked Vernon how many people in her life had been afflicted with MS. She said she did not know of many. I then advised Vernon that two of Delaney's former wives had acquired MS after being married to him and a third had a disability as well.

Vernon said, "Seriously?"

I asked Vernon if she had any medical or physical conditions. She said she had mild diabetes but it was treated with medication.

Vernon asked how Delaney could have done anything to Deborah if he had been so disabled by the stroke. I told her that perhaps Delaney was not as disabled as he let on.

I then asked Vernon about she [sic] and Delaney's sex life. I told Vernon that Delaney had previously told us that he could not perform sexually because of a medical issue.

Vernon told us that she and Delaney had a healthy sex life and that he had no problem performing.

Vernon said Delaney told her that Deborah was "into drugs" before they met and "that maybe she got back into that."

I asked Vernon how likely that a 55 year old woman, with no history of drug use, some disabilities and in a long term marriage would suddenly start using drugs and fall in with the "wrong people" would be.

Vernon said that this would not be very likely.

Bill Delaney agreed to sit down and talk with Peoria police. Before they met with him, police consulted FBI behavioral experts. The FBI used information received from people who knew Bill, previous interviews with him, and his postings on social media to come up with a profile.

The FBI concluded Bill Delaney had a personality disorder marked by:

- A lack of empathy for his victims
- A total lack of personal insight
- A habit of chronic lying
- No remorse
- A total lack of impulse control
- Likely to engage in high risk, self-destructive behaviors
- Likely to practice sado-masochistic behavior
- Likely to abandon family and jobs
- Potential to commit multiple acts of fraud, deceit, blatant abuse of others, and manipulation of others.

In other words, Bill Delaney was a psychopath.

Based on the information, Peoria police knew he was not likely to admit killing Debbie—even when presented with evidence linking him to the crime.

Investigators thought if they engaged him in conversation, and confronted him with known facts, he would continue to spin lies and would manufacture new ones. Which is what he did.

During their next interview with him, he confessed to some lies he had told—he admitted he hadn't served in the military—but persisted in some, including that Debbie had left him suddenly.

The police decided to see how he might respond to some "what ifs," some alternatives to what may have happened to Debbie. They asked him if she had died during rough sex or as a result of an overdose, and if he had panicked and disposed of the body. He said no.

Delaney was asked directly if he killed Debbie and he stated, "I could never do something like that." Delaney continually denied killing Debbie but agreed that she was most likely dead.

Circumstantial evidence began to pile up. When Bill learned that police were seizing his computer, he said they would find a copy of the typed, unsigned letter that Debbie supposedly left behind after moving out. He couldn't explain how he had suffered injuries on his hands and arms from cactus thorns at about the time Debbie disappeared. He finally said he had been hiking in the desert the day before Easter. Bill stated that he had nothing to do with Debbie being "missing"—but also stated that she "can't be found."

They cautioned Bill that they would probably be back to arrest him. Then they finished executing search warrants on his fifth wheeler and truck. Judy Vernon decided *not* to take Bill back to Missouri with her and police helped her pack up to leave.

On his computers they found a note he had written when Debbie disappeared, indicating he had considered committing suicide. Mostly they found—in his musings and on-line postings—a whole lot of contradictions, about their marriage, his military and work history, and Debbie's "leaving."

Bill Delaney had rarely told the truth—to his four wives, his new girlfriend, the men and women he worked with, the police, or to himself.

ON MAY 9, 2012 JUST AS DETECTIVES WERE IN THE process of preparing to arrest Bill Delaney, they got a call from a detective in the Coconino County Sheriff's Office. A citizen had called 911 after seeing a man slumped over inside a red Dodge pickup truck. Bill Delaney had shot himself in the head while sitting in his vehicle at the Mormon Lake Overlook outside of Flagstaff. The revolver was still in his right hand.

Det. Chris Boughey said Bill knew he was about to be arrested.

"I think our parting words to Mr. Delaney, when we left Tuba City, in the first part of May was, 'next time we see you we're putting handcuffs on you for killing your wife,'" Boughey said.

Police didn't know the exact reason why Bill Delaney took his life; they speculate that he may have believed evidence had been found implicating him in his wife's disappearance and death. He certainly knew he was the focus of the investigation and that he was likely to be indicted for murder.

After Bill Delaney's suicide, investigators continued to study items they had found, hoping for a clue to where he had left Debbie's body.

They found sexually explicit photographs, and numerous photographs of Bill wearing a bra and panties and posing in what appeared to be a hotel room. He had several online accounts with adult oriented web sites aimed at persons interested in finding other people interested in bondage and S&M.

What they never found was anything that pointed to what had happened to Debbie. They kept looking.

WHEN HIKERS FOUND SKELETAL REMAINS IN THE desert in February, 2013 police matched Debbie Delaney's dental records to the skull. They were lucky they could. Bill Delaney had so spectacularly removed any trace of her from their home that there was no DNA found to use for comparison. What could not be determined was how she died.

Police say they're certain Bill Delaney was responsible for the murder of Debbie.

Now they're looking at whether he also killed his third wife, Jayme, whose death in 2001 was ruled a suicide.

Freed—But Are They Innocent?

ONE DAY BILL MACUMBER WAS A FORTY-YEAR-OLD supervisor at a Honeywell factory that made computer parts. The next day he was a suspect in the murder of a young couple.

A towering six-feet, seven-inches, he liked to fish and attend baseball games. He had a home in Phoenix, three young sons, and a troubled marriage.

And then his wife, Carol Kempfert, told the Maricopa County Sheriff's Office—where she happened to work—that her husband had confessed to an unsolved crime, the killing of a young man and woman in the Arizona desert in 1962.

In 1975, Macumber, with no history of violence and continuing to maintain his innocence, was convicted of the murders of Tim McKillop and Joyce Sterrenberg.

In 1990, Debra Milke was a twenty-six year old single mother raising her four-year old son, Christopher. She occasionally had help from her roommate, Jim Styers, who had a young daughter. After she was convicted of arranging for Styers and his friend Roger Scott to kill Christopher in exchange for part of a measly five thousand dollars in life insurance, she became the first woman sentenced to death in Arizona in sixty years.

They are two of Arizona's most sensational murder cases, both with unexpected outcomes. After spending decades in prison, both Macumber and Milke were freed, but not necessarily because they are innocent.

Both went to prison based on unsubstantiated confessions. Macumber's wife claimed he had confessed to killing the young couple. Detective Armando Saldate claimed Milke had confessed to him that she had hired the murder of her son.

For decades those so-called confessions—and shaky forensic evidence in both cases—kept Macumber and Milke locked up.

Their release from prison—Macumber after nearly forty years, Milke after twenty-three years on death row—is controversial. Family members of their victims—and some of their own family members who helped send them to prison—are convinced that two killers have been let loose.

Have they?

Less than a year after being released, one of them was back in prison.

BLACK AND WHITE PHOTOS SHOW THE CRIME SCENE as police found it on May 24, 1962. On a dirt road east of Scottsdale, the bodies of two young people, both twenty years old, are sprawled where they were shot and left for dead.

The day before, Tim McKillop had driven the 20 miles from Phoenix to Scottsdale to meet his girlfriend, Joyce Sterrenberg, who lived with her parents. Both worked for Mountain Bell Telephone, McKillop as a lineman and Sterrenberg as an operator.

They stayed and talked with her family for a while and had cake to celebrate her father's birthday. Then they left to get gas for her car, a white 1959 Chevrolet Impala.

"We won't be gone long," Joyce told her parents as they left the house.

Tim had a blonde crew cut and big ears. Joyce wore her brunette hair curly and short. They had been dating for seven months, were in love, and had just announced plans to marry the next April.

The gas station attendant remembered the tall, pretty girl in Capri pants and a yellow and white checkered shirt. He said he could see a little bit of her midriff when she walked around her car at the station.

The couple drove by some model homes, maybe dreaming of starting their lives. They stopped and bought a milkshake. Then they drove to the desert off Scottsdale Road. They followed a dirt track east, then pulled off in the darkness. The night was cool, the moon nearly full.

The next morning, a school bus full of children passing nearby spotted the car and the bodies. When deputies arrived they found McKillop on his right side, near the driver's side of the car. Sterrenberg was on her back, several feet away. Detectives concluded she had tried to escape. Tim's class ring was still on her index finger. Both had been shot twice in the head. Nothing had been taken and Tim's wallet was at the scene.

There were tire tracks of a second car, and police found four shell casings from a .45 automatic.

Was it a senseless lovers' lane killing? A gang out for a good time?

Five days after the murders, Tim McKillop and Joyce Sterrenberg were buried side-by-side in a plot in a west Phoenix cemetery.

Their shared tombstone reads: "Together forever."

THE CASE WENT COLD FOR TWELVE YEARS, UNTIL Carol Kempfert told her supervisors that her husband had confessed to the murders. Macumber was arrested a week later.

Evidence was sketchy. Macumber declined a polygraph test but agreed to have his house searched, his gun confiscated, and fingerprints taken. Investigators said a partial palm print from the car—discarded for more than a decade because it had been impossible to determine whether it was a palm print or fingerprint — matched perfectly with Macumber's palm. They said markings on bullet casings matched a part of the firing mechanism in a gun Macumber owned. Prosecutors argued that the physical evidence linked Macumber to the murder scene. Macumber was convicted in 1975, but the verdict was tossed out on appeal. Macumber was retried in 1976 and found guilty a second time and sentenced to life in prison.

Macumber's first jury never heard the confession of a woman named Linda Primrose who claimed to be a passenger in a car looking for drugs and an eyewitness to the shootings. She named the gunman as a man she knew as Ernie Salazar. Primrose told officers details they had never revealed to the newspaper. She knew how the victims were shot. She knew how the cars had pulled into the empty desert, her story matching the tire tracks. During Macumber's second trial, when attorneys were certain Primrose would raise a reasonable doubt about Macumber's guilt, she recanted her earlier story.

But then came a confession. During a different murder investigation, Ernie Valenzuela—who sometimes used the name of Ernie Salazar—confessed to his lawyer and doctors that he had committed the lovers' lane murders. The confession couldn't be disclosed because of confidentiality requirements. But after Valenzuela was murdered in prison, his attorney, now freed of attorney-client privilege, attempted to tell the sheriff's office of the confession. They didn't take it seriously.

During his many years locked up Macumber was a model prisoner, teaching computer skills, English and business classes to other inmates and establishing a Chamber of Commerce chapter at the prison. He was permitted to leave the prison hundreds of times alone to travel to Chamber events. He said it never occurred to him to "run." He staged an annual prison rodeo to raise money for charity. He wrote novels and poetry. The other inmates affectionately called him "Pops."

In 2003, the Arizona Justice Project contacted Macumber's son, Ron Kempfert (his mother had changed the names of the children after the divorce to her maiden name). Ron and his two brothers had grown up believing what their mother told them—their father was a vicious murderer. But Ron decided to hear what the Justice Project had to say. What they told him was that they believed his father was innocent and that he had been framed by his ex-wife, Ron's mother.

Carol Kempfert had gone to work at the Maricopa County Sheriff's office in 1973, as she and Macumber were well on the road to divorce. The position granted her access to evidence, case histories, and criminal records. A deputy later testified that prints in the lovers' lane case were kept where anyone could have had access. The bullets recovered from the scene were stored in an unlocked desk drawer.

Macumber's lawyers believed she had access to evidence in the then 12-year old cold case and had tampered with it.

It was around the time she started working for the MCSO that Bill Macumber started suspecting his wife of cheating on him. A co-worker told Macumber's lawyers that Carol was seeing *three* deputies on the side. She became the subject of an internal Sheriff's Department scandal related to her sex life.

The divorce had made her bitter. The worst Carol could say about Macumber was that he was a fine father but a "country bumpkin," but she dredged up anything she could that might implicate Macumber, including a story from about the time of the McKillop and Sterrenberg murders. One night Macumber had arrived home covered in blood, she told the Sheriff's Department. He said he had been on his way to a hunting club meeting when he saw a car on the side of a road with its hood up. He stopped to help and in return for his kindness was jumped by three teenage boys trying to rob him. One of the kids came at him with a pipe and he fought back. They both said the event happened sometime in the spring of 1962.

The Arizona Justice Project convinced Macumber's son Ron that his father was innocent and that his mother had framed him. Over the years, Macumber and his attorneys petitioned the Arizona Board of Executive Clemency unsuccessfully three times. When they petitioned a fourth time in 2009, the board unanimously recommended his sentence be commuted, a rare move, saying, "An injustice has been done in Mr. Macumber's case" and that his wife had "motive, means and opportunity to falsely pin the murders on Mr. Macumber."

Arizona Gov. Jan Brewer denied the recommendation for clemency.

In 2011, a trip to the hospital for a bowel obstruction turned into internal bleeding, a heart attack, and a coma. Before he emerged from critical condition, Bill Macumber had lost 32 pounds. The staff and volunteers of the Arizona Justice Project believed the man they had become attached to over the years was dying. So with no other options, on February 2, 2012, the project — citing Macumber's ill health — filed a last-ditch petition to get him released.

The state came back with a deal: Macumber would be released for time served if he pleaded no contest to the lovers' lane murders.

CHRISTOPHER CONAN MILKE HAD STRAIGHT GOLDEN hair, bangs that reached his big brown eyes, and a million dollar smile. At four, he seemed happy all the time. Despite his mother's financial struggles to make a life for the two of them, in photographs they both appear happy and close.

Debra Sadeik was born in Berlin, Germany, to a military family. In 1965 the family moved to the U.S., where Debra attended high school and college. She married Mark Milke in 1984 and gave birth to her son, Christopher Conan Milke, in 1985.

Debra was twenty-five years old and divorced from Christopher's dad, a former exotic dancer. On the day Christopher disappeared, December 2, 1989, Debra stayed at the apartment to do laundry while her roommate (who she knew through her sister) forty-two year old Jim Styers, took the boy to the Metrocenter Mall in Phoenix. Styers was a Vietnam veteran, unemployed, taking Lithium for depression, and infatuated with Milke. Christopher had begged to see

Santa Claus. Before finding Santa's village, the two made a stop in the men's bathroom in Sears. And that's when Styers said Christopher vanished. He notified mall security and called Debra, and she called 911.

The truth was that Christopher never came close to seeing Santa Claus. After leaving the apartment, Styers had picked up his friend, Roger Scott. They took Christopher for pizza, and then drove out into the desert, where one of the men shot him. Not surprisingly, they pointed the finger at each other.

After more than fourteen hours of interrogation, Scott admitted that he knew where Christopher was and that the boy was dead. He took the police to the desert north of Phoenix, where Christopher's body was discovered in a dry river bed. He had been shot three times in the head. According to the lead case detective Armando Saldate, Jr., - who became Debra Milke's nemesis—Scott claimed that Styers had committed the murder and that Milke had "wanted it done." Scott later repeated these accusations in a taped confession. "She just had to get away from him...she wasn't cut out to be a mother, and she wanted us to take care of it," Scott said.

Styers, who had helped in the initial search for Christopher, was arrested and interviewed by police after being implicated by Scott.

Milke voluntarily went to the Pinal County sheriff's office where she was interrogated by Det. Saldate. The interrogation was not recorded or witnessed by anyone other than the detective. Three days later, in a written report of the interrogation, Saldate indicated Milke had confessed to arranging the murder of her son Christopher.

Prosecutors called Milke the "puppeteer" and "mastermind" of her son's murder. They said she "had a way with the guys" and that Christopher may have gotten in the way of her relationships.

She was charged with conspiracy to commit first degree murder, kidnapping, child abuse, and first-degree murder. Prosecutors relied on the alleged confession and pointed out that Milke had taken out a $5,000 life insurance policy on her son. Her own sister and father testified that she had neglected Christopher, sometimes leaving him with friends for days at a time.

But there was no proof that Milke wanted to get rid of Christopher, or that she had asked Styers and Scott to kill the boy. Det. Saldate destroyed his original interview notes, and there was another problem—Milke had never signed a Miranda waiver, giving up her right to remain silent.

In October 1990, she was convicted of all charges and sentenced to death. Styers and Scott were charged and tried separately. Both were convicted of first degree murder and also received the death penalty. Forensics never proved who actually shot little Christopher three times in the head.

Then, in March, 2013, the U.S. Court of Appeals for the Ninth Circuit threw out Milke's conviction, ruling that she did not receive a fair trial. Milke's alleged confession, as reported by Det. Saldate, was the only direct evidence linking her to the crime. But the confession was only as good as Saldate's word. His interview with her was never recorded and there was no proof that she had confessed. Saldate's credibility became an issue.

The court held that Milke's rights had been violated by the failure to turn over Saldate's personnel file to the defense. That file included multiple instances of misconduct, including eight cases where confessions, indictments or convictions were thrown out because Saldate either lied under oath or violated the suspects' rights during interrogations.

WEARING A WESTERN-STYLE SHIRT, BOLO TIE, BLUE jeans and sneakers, an ailing Bill Macumber walked out of prison on November 7, 2012. He was seventy-seven years old and had missed out on decades of family events.

According to the judge who handed Macumber his freedom, it is not a clear-cut case of freeing an innocent man. "We will never know with certainty what happened on that 1962 night," Judge Bruce Cohen said in court. Maricopa County Attorney Bill Montgomery cautioned against saying Macumber had been exonerated. "He's not innocent," Montgomery said. "He's guilty."

The parents of Joyce Sterrenberg and Tim McKillop called it "tragic" that Macumber was released.

Macumber's ex-wife, Carol Kempfert, said she passed four lie detector tests when she was questioned by police and maintains that she never tampered with evidence.

She denied any wrongdoing in a *"Nightline"* interview.

"I didn't wake up one morning and say, 'Gee, I think I'll go frame my husband today,'" she told *"Nightline"*. "I did not manufacture, nor did I tamper with evidence, ever. And I passed four polygraphs, and I'll be happy to take another. I did not frame him, and he did admit it to me and he did do it, and the evidence was there.

"They need to know they just let a murderer loose," she continued."I feel sorry for the [victims'] families because I know they were unhappy with this, and all I can tell them is I did my best and it just didn't work, and I'm sorry for that."

At a press conference on the day he was released, a teary-eyed Macumber told reporters "Justice, however late, is still justice."

In an interview, Macumber said he did not blame the jury that found him guilty, given the evidence they heard and the evidence they *didn't* hear, that of Vanzuela's confession. "They had to convict," he said. "I understand their decision."

He pledged to help the Arizona Justice Project, his "second family," review cases of other older inmates. "They're all elderly. They've all done 30 or more years. They pose no threat to society whatsoever. Why not put them back with their families?

"The world has passed me by in four decades," he said."I am not interested in totally catching up, but I will catch up in the degree that I have to. I am computer literate, I am going to get on the internet and go to work."

When he was released, it was the first time in nearly forty years Macumber could see his children (two of his three sons remain estranged), grandchildren, and great-grandchildren, sip a beer, take in a baseball game, and go fishing. He had emphysema, arthritis and heart trouble. He had a dry cough and wheezed in between his words, but still rolled his own cigarettes, a few a day. He enjoyed looking out at the world.

"Nature is such a wonderful phenomenon and too many people fail to enjoy it like they should. I sit here and look the window for hours at a time."

His freedom didn't last.

ON SEPTEMBER 6, 2013, FORTY-NINE YEAR OLD Debra Milke, her once-brown hair now gray, walked out of the Perryville state prison complex in Goodyear, Arizona where she had spent 23 years on death row. She hugged her terminally ill mother for the first time in decades.

Six months earlier, a court of appeals had thrown out her conviction, saying she did not receive a fair trial. One investigator called her case "the most disgraceful police work I've ever seen."

In January, 2014, a judge denied a motion to dismiss the murder charge against her. Milke's future remains uncertain while prosecutors plan to re-try her in 2015.

Her ex-husband, Arizona Milke, has no doubt that she arranged to have Christopher killed. But he also thinks she'll be acquitted at the next trial. Prosecutors are again seeking the death penalty but he doesn't want to see her executed."Christopher came out of her -- I don't want to see her killed," he said.

Milke's friends and supporters, both in the U.S. and in her native Germany, bought a house for her to live in while she awaits her re-trial.

James Styers and Roger Scott remain on Arizona's death row.

For both Bill Macumber and Debra Milke, the so-called confessions that first imprisoned them have now freed them.

Milke is free—for now—because of a confession she says she never made to a detective with a history of police misconduct.

Bill Macumber's so-called confession to his wife is, along with lack of forensic evidence, one reason Arizona released him.

Some people still believe Bill Macumber and Debra Milke are guilty of their crimes.

They are free—but may or may not be innocent.

Afterword

IN OCTOBER, 2013 LESS THAN A YEAR AFTER BILL Macumber—model prisoner, public speaker, subject of a prize-winning book and documentary—was released from prison, he was arrested and charged with sexually assaulting two girls. The Arizona Republic reported that the victims were young relatives of the 78-year old Macumber. It quoted the son he had reunited with, Ron Macumber, who had taken his father's name again, as saying he had kicked his father out of his house in Colorado after accusations arose that he may have been sexually abusing young relatives.

"It makes me angry to no end, for the 12 years I spent to get him out of jail, to do what he did," Ronald Macumber told the newspaper."When he's found guilty, he can rot in prison. He's lost everything as far as I'm concerned.

"I believe he's still innocent of the murders," he went on to say, "but I know for a fact he's not the man I thought he was."

The girls told police that Macumber touched them inappropriately multiple times under their clothes and underwear when they sat on his lap.

Macumber denies the sex abuse allegations. He is in jail awaiting trial.

The Vicious Vixen
By Stephanie Cook

"AFTER ALL THE LIES YOU HAVE TOLD, WHY SHOULD we believe you now?" Maricopa County (Ariz.) Superior Court Judge Sherry Stephens read the jury's question aloud, then peered over toward the witness stand.

She was waiting for an answer from Jodi Arias. With her long hair now darkened, wearing little or no makeup and with large, unflattering eyeglasses framing her face, Arias seemed like a different woman from the sexy blonde who posed wearing a bikini in a photograph with the boyfriend she was charged with viciously killing, Travis Alexander.

The sudden change in her appearance seemed calculated—she would do whatever she needed to do to be taken as something other than the sexually obsessed vixen portrayed in the media. Travis' friends thought she enjoyed being on the stand and being in the spotlight. So did others.

Under a rare law in Arizona, juries can quiz defendants through written questions read aloud by a judge. During one long week of her trial in March, 2013, Jodi Arias answered hundreds of such questions. It was clear from the questions—and shots of the skeptical faces of the four women and eight men shown during TV coverage—that the jury didn't believe her defense.

But Jodi, poised, rehearsed, playing the part of the wronged woman pushed to violence, turned to speak to the jury and answered:

"The lies that I've told in this case can be tied directly back to either protecting Travis' reputation or my involvement in his death."

Even when she admitted she had lied and she had killed Travis, the jury didn't know what to make of her.

Any case involving an attractive young woman accused of murder is likely to make headlines, but this case had it all: sex, jealousy, and the Mormon Church. The 34-year old former waitress and amateur photographer became famous overnight for the brutal death of her on-again, off-again lover.

Rather than hide from the spotlight once authorities named her as the primary suspect, Jodi fanned the flames of what would become an all-out media explosion by sitting for interviews with "48 Hours" and "Inside Edition." When her murder trial finally began in December, 2012, it seemed the whole country was watching. Every moment of testimony was streamed for the public on YouTube, live-tweeted by reporters, and dissected by cable personalities including HLN's Nancy Grace. And because everything is recorded these days and little is kept private, the jury heard phone calls of the couple's conversations about their most lurid sexual fantasies.

The jury charged with deciding her fate would have to do so under a microscope, and Jodi Arias, the only living witness to the murder she'd been accused of, had a story that just didn't seem to add up.

She claimed that after a day of sex and naked photo shoots, she'd dropped Travis' expensive new camera while getting shots of him in his shower. When he flew into a violent rage and lunged at her, she responded in self-defense. But did self-defense require 27 stab wounds, near decapitation, and a gunshot to the head?

If ever there was a case of overkill, it was the murder of Travis Alexander.

Born in Riverside, California, Travis Victor Alexander and his seven siblings suffered and starved through their youth. With an absent father, they depended hopelessly on a drug-addicted mother who teetered between bouts of rage and neglect, often sleeping for days on end while her children scrounged for food and fended off hordes of roaches. In a blog posting in 2008, Travis wrote about the abuse he suffered at home, and how it affected his social life at school.

"...School wasn't much better, when your clothes are as dirty as the rest of you and you stink and have lice you don't make a ton of friends. Sadly as you could imagine I was mocked for my. Nothing too harsh, no where close to what was said at home. I will not give much detail on that as I feel it is inappropriate to state. I will say though I have never heard in any movie, on any street corner, or amongst the vilest of men any string of words so offensive and hateful, said with such disgust as was the words that my mother said to my sisters and I."

Travis' life turned around the day his grandmother took him and his siblings in. She saved him from the torments of his mother and introduced him to The Church of Jesus Christ of Latter-day Saints. He eventually settled down in Mesa, Arizona, where he seemed to be a respected member of the Mormon Church—despite his violation of church tenets on pre-marital sex. He worked as a legal insurance salesman and motivational speaker.

Like Travis, Jodi Ann Arias was born in California. She grew up in the small town of Yreka, and in her interview with "48 Hours," Jodi called her childhood "almost ideal." Once the trial rolled around, Jodi's story predictably changed. She claimed that both of her parents abused her while growing up. Maybe she really was the victim of abuse, or maybe she got the idea from Travis' own traumatic upbringing. For Jodi, the past is like an Etch a Sketch: each time she goes back to it, she just wipes it clean and creates something new.

The few facts that have remained consistent about Jodi's life are that she dropped out of high school before her senior year and worked odd jobs waitressing to pay the bills. Her dream was to make it as a professional photographer, but during her late twenties she began looking for success in sales with Prepaid Legal Services, the same company that employed Travis.

The pair met at a Las Vegas conference in 2006 and sparks flew immediately. Travis was 31, and Jodi was 28. Despite the geographical distance between them—Travis living in Arizona, Jodi in California—the two talked constantly—exchanging more than 82,000 emails during their two-year relationship. Only two months after they met, Travis baptized Jodi into the Mormon Church. (She would testify that Travis' way of getting around the Church's prohibition of premarital sex was to indulge primarily in oral and anal sex. In fact, she said that she and Travis had anal sex the same day as the baptism.)

But just as quickly as they jumped into their relationship, they jumped out of it. Jodi caught Travis talking to other women, and by late June, only four months after they began dating, Travis and Jodi split up. Travis began seeing another women, and it seemed he'd quickly moved on. But Jodi hadn't. Rather than maintain her distance from the man who had wronged her, Jodi relocated from California to a neighborhood—one not far from Travis' in Mesa, Arizona.

TRAVIS' NEW GIRLFRIEND WAS 19 YEAR OLD LISA Andrews, who he met at church. Shortly after they began dating, odd events began to happen. Travis found his tires slashed and Lisa received a threatening and disturbing email:

> *"You are a shameful whore. Your Heavenly Father must be deeply ashamed of the whoredoms you've committed with that insidious man. If you let him stay in your bed one more time or even sleep under the same roof as him, you will be giving the appearance of evil."*

While the email was signed, "John Doe," Travis told friends he suspected Jodi was the culprit. Quickly she became known as Travis' "stalker ex-girlfriend." In investigator's notes made after the murder, one of Travis' roommates mentioned how Jodi never really stopped hanging around, even crawling into their rented house through the dog door on occasion, the door Travis' pug mix, Napoleon, used.

Travis may have felt genuinely threatened or creeped out by Jodi at times, but unbeknownst to his friends, he maintained a sexual relationship with his former girlfriend long after they'd publicly broken up. In January, only a month after Lisa received the unsettling email, Jodi sent flirtatious text messages to Travis' phone. At least one of the messages implied that Travis had texted Jodi first: *"Ahhh!! I fell asleep! But to answer your question, yes I want to grind you. And I want to be LOUD..."* Jodi wrote.

Lisa Andrews didn't like the way Jodi was always around, and when she caught Travis cheating with Jodi, Lisa and Travis went their separate ways. Unfortunately for Jodi, Lisa was only one of the several women Travis flirted with or dated while sleeping with her.

In March 2008 Jodi and Travis went on a road trip together. They posed for pictures in front of a Mormon temple in Oklahoma City, OK and a statue in Amarillo, TX, almost like they were a couple again. But soon after, Jodi decided it was finally time to have some space and she moved back to California. It looked like all of the ups and downs of an increasingly dark relationship between the pair might finally be over. Travis took to his blog, writing about his ambitions and hopes for the year to come. He finished the entry writing:

> *"This year will be the best year of my life and I will succeed!"*

But Travis would always be distracted by young women. He met Marie Hall—known as Mimi—at church. Mimi and Travis became close and Travis invited her to accompany him on a business trip to Mexico. She agreed—as long as they went on a purely friendly basis. Meanwhile, Jodi, who had hoped to go on the trip, found out that he was taking another woman. That's when she set in motion her plan to get even.

Staying sexually involved with Travis—and knowing she could never really have him—was driving Jodi mad.

ON MAY 26, A WEEK BEFORE TRAVIS WAS FOUND dead, he and Jodi came to verbal blows like never before. However the fight started, it ended with Travis berating Jodi in a string of text and instant messages full of hatred and rage:

"I sent you a response to your dire conversation that I hope you read because you need to read it. Maybe it will spark human emotion in you, something that only seems to exist when it comes to your own problems. But everyone else is just a part of your sick agenda. By the way your pic comment to Danny Jones makes you look like a pure whore, even more to the people who know you. You should be embarrassed by it. If he knew what I knew about you he'd spit in ur face...I don't want your apology I want you to understand what I think of you. I want you to understand how evil I think you are. You are the worst thing that ever happened to me."

Old habits die hard, and even with new love interests and 1,000 miles separating them, Jodi and Travis couldn't escape the ugly pattern of hateful fights and torrid sexual rendezvous they'd grown accustomed to. A few days after their venomous text exchange, Travis and Jodi had agreed to meet at his home in Mesa.

On May 28, there was a theft at Jodi's grandparent's home in Yreka, where she was living. In addition to a stereo and DVD player, $30 in cash was missing—and a .25 caliber gun. (A .25 caliber bullet round was later found at the murder scene but the gun has never been recovered.) Jodi embarked on a road trip a few days later, saying she was planning to visit friends around California and then head to Jordon, Utah to visit Ryan Burns, a man who she had developed a long-distance flirtation with since meeting him at a conference earlier in the year.

Only she knew she also planned to visit Travis.

In an attempt to cover her tracks, she went out of her way to rent a car and borrowed two gas cans from an ex-boyfriend in Monterey before heading off. She was avoiding leaving a credit card trail.

At 4 a.m. on June 4, 2008, Jodi arrived at Travis' home and found him watching YouTube videos on his laptop. The couple took a nap, and then got down to business. According to Jodi, Travis tied her to the bed using a rope, and then used a kitchen knife to make it just the right length. They spent the day having sex and taking nude photos of one another using Travis' camera. In court, Jodi testified that after ejaculating on her back at one point, Travis made her feel "used" by telling her to go clean herself up. Later, it was Travis' turn to shower.

Unlike Jodi, he didn't make it out alive.

Moments before Jodi Arias shot him, slit his throat from ear to ear, and stabbed him in the heart, she snapped a few final photos of Travis Alexander.

In most of the pictures taken by Jodi, he poses awkwardly as water runs down his chest and back. In a final shot of his face, Travis stares directly into the camera, his brows furrowed in an expression that can be interpreted as a slightly pudgy-faced young man posing—or as a look of fear.

Moments later the camera seems to have fallen, misfiring and capturing a woman's dark figure standing over her battered prey.

While Travis' blood circled down the drain, Jodi drove barefoot through the desert. She pulled over to rinse her arms and legs and change clothes, and did some other tidying up. She claimed to have no memory of what happened to the gun and knife used to kill Travis, or the rope they used as a sex toy, yet she thought to call her dead ex-lover's phone four times as a ruse.

The next day she finally met up with Ryan Burns in Jordan, arriving several hours late with cuts on her hands. Jodi and Ryan attended business meetings and engaged in heated make out sessions before Jodi got back on the road. Finally, on June 7, she arrived in Redding to return the rental car. According to agents, the car was missing floor mats and had red stains on the seats. The vehicle was cleaned before the police knew of it.

On June 9, Mimi became concerned that she hadn't heard from Travis. They should be getting ready for their trip to Mexico, right? She went to Travis' house, but no one seemed to be home so Mimi called her friends, Michelle Lowery and Dallin Forrest, to help her. No one answered when they knocked on the door, but they obtained the garage key code from another friend. Once inside they found Travis' roommate, Zachary Billings, in his room with his girlfriend. Travis and his roommates weren't close, and it was common for Travis to leave town without saying anything, so no one had noticed anything odd.

Napoleon, Travis' dog, was loose downstairs. Travis' bedroom door was locked so Zach went rummaging for a spare key. Mimi and Zach's girlfriend, Amanda, stayed in the hall while Zach and Dallin went inside. The bed was unmade and there was an empty black camera bag on the floor. They continued through the room and as they neared Travis' bathroom they saw blood—lots of blood. Travis was in his shower, battered and decomposing. Their friend was dead.

When Mesa police detective Esteban Flores arrived at the crime scene, one name was on everyone's lips. Flores wrote in his incident report:

> *"Before we could determine what had happened to Travis, the subjects on scene had begun to mention the name, Jodi Arias. They told officers that if someone had done harm to Travis, we needed to look at Jodi Arias as an investigative lead."*

When police found Travis, he had been dead five days. They said the stench was overwhelming.

His roommates hadn't noticed.

BETWEEN 2008 AND HER TRIAL IN 2012, JODI WOULD change her story as easily as she'd changed her hair from blonde to brunette. Even the most open-minded court-watchers (and there were millions watching the coverage on cable television) believed her make-over was deliberate. She now looked mousy, not at all like a vixen.

When police first questioned her, Jodi swore she was never even in Mesa, but investigators had Jodi's bloody palm print at the scene. When journalists interviewed her before her trial, Jodi spun a harrowing tale of her escape after two intruders broke into Travis' home and attacked him. Unfortunately, Jodi couldn't explain why she left her lover and friend dying without ever calling the police, or why investigators recovered photos of Jodi standing over Travis' body on his camera, which she had tried to hide in his washing machine.

Finally, when she made it to trial, Jodi admitted to murdering Travis, but said she did so after years of verbal and mental abuse. She recalled conversations that proved her point—but they happened to be ones that weren't recorded. She recalled injuries sustained during Travis' bouts of rage over the years—but she'd never photographed them. And those details about what happened in the moments during and immediately after the murder—the facts she just couldn't explain away—Jodi testified that she'd forgotten them all after entering a fear-induced fog during the ordeal.

JODI ARIAS WAS STRUNG ALONG, USED, AND IF NOT physically, then certainly mentally abused. As a willing partner she helped Travis Alexander play out his most deviant sexual fantasies and then watched him hand out his affections to other women. She was heartbroken and hurt, and probably deserved better.

Heartbreak or not, a dead man demands justice, and on May 8, 2013 a jury of her peers convicted Jody Arias of first-degree murder. While they agreed to Jodi's guilt, the jury could not reach a consensus on sentencing. A requirement of the death penalty in Arizona is premeditation, and the jury couldn't agree that she had planned Travis' death.

There have been at least fourteen books written about Jodi Arias and one made-for-television movie. But the media circus didn't end with her conviction.

In the fall of 2014, Jodi Arias faced round two, the penalty phase of her murder trial.

There are only two possible outcomes. She could be sentenced to life in prison with a chance of parole after 25 years, or she could be sentenced to death.

Afterword

SOME OF THE 400 QUESTIONS THE JURY PUT TO JODI Arias during her 2013 trial:

Q: Why did you put the camera in the washer?

A: I don't have memory of that. I don't know why I would do that.

Q: Did you ever take pictures of yourself after he hit you?

A: No, I did not.

Q: Did Travis' closet doors have locks on them?

A: I don't remember them having any locks.

Q: If not, how did you have time to get the gun down if he was right behind you?

A: I don't remember if he was right behind me or not. I just had a sense that he was chasing me.

Q: Did you record other phone sex conversations?

A: Yes Q: Why did you feel so uncomfortable about anal sex with Travis, when you had previously tried it?

A: In my previous relationships, it was only something we had tried one time, maybe two. And those were long term relationships, it was not a part of the "bedroom curriculum" because it was uncomfortable. That was Travis' preference and I got the KY to make it less uncomfortable.

Q: You told (another man) that you wanted to abstain from sex until marriage. If that was the case, then why have sex with Travis?

A: Travis explained it to me that vaginal sex was off limits, and everything else was not as egregious to that law.

Q: You testified that Travis gave you The Book of Mormon at Starbucks. Did you read it thoroughly? If so, when?

A: I did read it thoroughly. I attempted to read one chapter a day. I think I finished it in about 8 months. Also read it in 2008, 2009, 2010 a chapter a day, starting in January. I haven't done it since.

Q: Does the Book of Mormon go into detail about the Vow of Chasity?

A: Doesn't go into explicit detail, it uses verbiage such as whoredoms, things like that, "being unclean" in reference to sexual sin. It does reference those things that are considered sinful.

Q: Were you paid for the interview with "48 Hours"?

A: No, no, I never asked for compensation, and they never offered.

Q: Were you paid for the interview with "Inside Edition"?

A: The same, no. Someone encouraged me to ask because they had paid her $50, but I did not ask.

Q: You mentioned an earlier failed attempt using rope during a sexual encounter. Can you tell us what happened that day, when this occurred, and how Travis handled the failure?

A: Yes, he handled it just fine, he didn't get upset, we just stopped, we used twine, and it was scratchy, and not cutting my wrists, but abrasive, somewhat painful, at that point he just cut the twine off with a knife as well.

Q: Did Travis' dog usually bark when someone came into the house?

A: Yes, if the dog heard the door open, he was very animated. Would bark very loud.

Q: Did the dog usually bark with loud unexplained noises?

A: Typically, only if the doorbell rang or someone knocked at the front door.

Q: Why would you stay with someone who had sex with you while you were sleeping?

A: At that point, May 2007, I was in love with Travis, and it didn't make a difference to me, honestly. I was in love with him, my only concern, was I believed from a spiritual and religious perspective, I believed our relationship would not be blessed if we acted that way, as in vaginal sex. That was my belief at the time.

Q: When did you find out that Travis had a gun?

A: I found out in fall of 2007, when I was cleaning his shelves, I had different projects, and it was around the fall, I don't remember if it was October or November, but it was around that time.

Q: To your knowledge, did police ever find your grandfather's gun that was stolen?

A: To my knowledge, no, none of the property that was stolen from the house was recovered.

Q: Why did you place Travis' body back in the shower?

A: I could only speculate, because I don't remember. I could speculate on who that I know I am, or thought I was.

Q: You say Travis' had attacked you before June 2008, but would apologize to you after he did it, so why was the June 4, 2008 incident so different?

A: June 4th was escalated and he always apologized afterward on prior occasions, on prior occasions I never feared for my life, and even when he was choking me out and I was losing conscienceless, I didn't have time to fear for my life, I passed out. It wasn't until after that incident, when I reflected back on it, I realized I could have died. If he could take it that far, and he was as angry as he was, I perceived very clearly that he was trying to get back on top of me again and that freaked me out, I was scared out of my mind.

Q: You and Travis' continued to talk on the phone, after you moved back to Yreka, including phone sex. Would it be fair to say, you were upset that he was taking another woman to Cancun?

A: Ummmm, No! Um, I was not upset, I wasn't upset at all actually. Cancun was planned almost a year before. He was taking a babysitter I thought. I didn't learn that he was taking Mimi Hall until long afterwards.

Q: Why did you take the rope and gun with you?

A: There were a lot of actions I took that day, that I don't remember, um, but as far as disposing of it, I knew that something bad had happened. I knew that something, I felt that I had done something wrong.

Q: Did you try and clean up the scene after you left on June 4, 2008?

A: Based on the evidence, I believe I did um, maybe make some kind of attempt, but I don't recall doing that.

Q: After you shot Travis, why not run out of the house to get away?

A: Initially that was my attempt, that's why I started running down the hall, the bedroom doors were closed.

Objection - In her earlier statement she said after she shot him, she didn't remember.

A: No, I said it got foggy after I shot him.

Overruled, you may continue.

A: Maybe I misunderstood the question, I thought you meant after I got body slammed, is that ...

Judge repeats question.

A: Okay, I'm sorry, that is correct, after I shot him, I didn't know I had shot him, but after the gun went off, he lunged. After he lunged at me, we fell over, and he was trying to get on top of me. It's hard to describe the fear. It was like mortal terror, it really was, he was trying to get on top of me, and then he threatened my life, I thought he had intentions to kill me. So, I don't remember any specifics, of what happened right after that point.

Q: Why didn't you call 911?

A: I was very scared of what would happen to me. I was scared at that point of what was going to happen. I knew that, well I felt that I had done something wrong. I don't really have an adequate explanation for my state of mind, I just know, I knew that something really bad had happened, and I was scared.

Q: If Travis attacked you on June 4th, why not just tell the police the truth from the start?

A: That one is kind of a complicated answer, I didn't want people to know the kinds of things that were going on in our relationship. I felt that if I told police that Travis attacked me, I would have to give an explanation of why he attacked me. I would have to go back through the different incidents we had gone through, and how those things didn't really begin until I walked in on him. I believe they were related, and I didn't ever want to go there. So it was all convoluted, and I thought by saying that, I thought that would open the door to that, to that, to that, and I didn't want to disedify him, I didn't want, was embarrassed about a lot of those things, and ashamed. I was also very scared about, whether I was defending myself or not. I felt like it was wrong to kill somebody, regardless of the circumstances.

The Deadly Daughter-in-Law

DORIS ANN CARLSON WAS JUST AN EVIL CAREGIVER—short-tempered, resentful, greedy—before she became a murdering one.

For a while she was on a gravy train—one supplied by her mother-in-law, Mary Lynne Carlson. Lynne Carlson, fifty-three, was a former beautician with multiple sclerosis who lived with her son, twenty-four year old David and his thirty-four year old wife, Doris.

The couple definitely got the best of the arrangement. After David and Doris moved to Arizona from Illinois, Lynne Carlson put $70,000 toward a house in Peoria, a suburb of Phoenix, for them to live in together. In return for giving her very little care, and grudgingly at that, the couple received $850 a month from Lynne to pay for food and utility bills. Lynne could also draw from another fund, when necessary. All in all, her annuities and a trust fund totaled about a quarter of a million dollars.

As her only child, David was the beneficiary of her money. His wife Doris was an invalid's worst nightmare. A scruffy, 220 pound woman with long auburn hair and big eyeglasses, she was impatient with her mother-in-law, claimed Lynne was only *pretending* to have MS, yelled and cursed at her, and more than once suggested to her husband that they kill her to get her money.

In July, 1996, Lynne needed more care than her son and daughter-in-law could even pretend to provide and she moved into a residential care facility. She told her conservator that she was afraid to stay in the house because of the seedy men Doris and David rented rooms to—20-year old John Daniel McReaken and 17-year old Scott Smith. She mentioned she was tired of paying the bills for all of them and never received any of the money Doris got for renting rooms.

When Lynne moved into the nursing home, David and Doris stopped receiving her monthly annuity and were broke. That fall, Doris asked McReaken if he knew anyone who would kill her mother-in-law for $20,000. McReaken brought Smith into the deal, offering to split the fee with him. Doris gave them money to buy gloves. They already had knives, the butterfly folding type traditionally made in the Philippines that are illegal in some countries and many U.S. states.

But before Doris and David had Lynne Carlson killed, they went to visit her in the nursing home one last time. They asked her to sign over some money to them so they wouldn't lose the house. She refused saying she would have to talk to her financial advisor.

The next evening, McReaken and Smith dressed in black, got out their knives, and pulled on their new gloves. Just after one a.m. on October 25, 1996 Doris gave them a key to her mother-in-law's room and drove to a grocery store parking lot near the nursing home. While she waited for them the two men walked to the nursing facility and entered her unit. Smith stayed in the living room disconnecting the television and moving things around to make it look like a burglary. McReaken went into Lynne's bedroom, hesitated, closed his eyes, and stabbed her eight to ten times in the throat and upper body. When the men got back to the car, Doris asked if Lynne was dead. McReaken assured her she was.

At five a.m. a nursing assistant checked on Lynne. The wounded woman was able to call out for help and tell her that she had tried to fight "them" off. She underwent several surgeries but never recovered and died six months after the stabbing. She was never able to speak with the police about what happened.

DORIS AND DAVID WERE NOTHING IF NOT BRAZEN. They must have been shocked that Lynne hadn't died during the attack and afraid that she would wake up and talk. From the start, the police focused on the couple. They found Lynne Carlson's blood in Doris' car and got a major break when a "friend" of the suspects came forward and told them McReaken had confessed to him about the stabbing. The police set up a sting. They put a microphone in the friend's car and recorded both Smith and McReaken talking about the stabbing and how much money they were supposed to get.

While Lynne was hospitalized and undergoing surgeries, David and Doris visited her in the hospital. Less than a month after the attack they were at her bedside when—like a scene from a movie—the police arrived and arrested them for attempted murder. The hospital staff applauded as the couple was led away. They had always been suspicious of David and Doris.

McReaken and Scott were arrested, too. All four admitted their involvement in the attack. Doris said she wanted to use her mother-in-law's money to try and get custody of her three children—two from another marriage and one from a prior relationship. The charges became murder when Lynne Carlson died April 21, 1997.

The wheels of justice turned slowly. It was more than two years after the murder before Doris Carlson stood trial.

Prosecutors claimed Doris was the mastermind behind the murder plot. They told the jury how the victim was helplessly mutilated and how senseless the crime was. On July 27, 1999, a jury found Carlson guilty of first-degree murder, conspiracy to commit first-degree murder, and first-degree burglary. Eight months later the judge determined there would be no leniency for Doris Ann Carlson and sentenced her to death. She was just the fourth woman in Arizona history to face execution.

David Carlson received a life sentence for conspiracy to commit murder. Dan McReaken was given a life sentence for first-degree murder, and Scott Smith was sentenced to ten years in prison for essentially serving as the lookout.

In 2002, after hearing an appeal, Arizona's Supreme Court reduced Doris Carlson's sentence to life without the possibility of parole. The court decided that there was a disparity between her sentence and those the men received. Neither McReaken, who stabbed the victim, nor the man who stood to inherit the money, David Carlson, were sentenced to death. And there was the matter of the public defender who represented Doris.

Her name was Carmen Fischer and at the time of Doris Carlson's trial Fischer was beginning to make the kind of news an attorney should never make. In July 1999, the same month Doris was on trial for capital murder, the Arizona State Bar filed a formal complaint against Fischer for having an intimate relationship with a client, convicted killer Michael Sanders. According to

Carlson's appeal, several of the jurors on Carlson's case had read coverage of Fischer's affair with Sanders, who was accused of a double homicide during a home-invasion robbery.

Fischer and Sanders were caught hugging and kissing. News accounts told of Fischer wearing short skirts for the benefit of her client, and they salaciously quoted jail reports of the lawyer having her skirt hiked up as Sanders leaned toward her and reached between her legs. There was even some videotape of one incident that made the rounds on local TV. Fischer was booted from the case as a public defender but was allowed to represent Sanders as a private attorney.

The public was outraged. At the time, the State Bar of Arizona did not have a specific rule against clients and counselors being intimate, although conflict-of-interest rules supposedly covered such improprieties (the State Bar finally adopted such a rule in 2003). The Bar brought a complaint against Fischer, but she beat the rap, with the hearing officer ruling that she had been tried by "jailhouse rumors" and that the Bar had been unable to substantiate its claims against her.

The record of the complaint was expunged, and Fischer's legal slate remained clean until another incident. In 2011, she married Angel Lopez Garcia, an alleged leader of the New Mexican Mafia, a much-feared, prison-based Latino gang infamous for running drugs and ordering hits from inside. The bride was 56 at the time, the groom 32. Garcia's rap sheet included a drive-by shooting, various gang-related and drug charges as well as charges stemming from his involvement in a car chase that led to a Phoenix cop being shot through the neck.

By October, 2013, Carmen Fischer, like her husband, was behind bars, charged with 47 counts of fraud and money laundering. In March, 2014, Carmen Fisher was sentenced to three years in prison and four years of probation. Her LinkedIn profile still lists her as a practicing attorney in Arizona.

David Carlson is serving a life term at Arizona's Louis prison in Buckeye. Dan McReaken—known as John in Arizona prison records—is serving a life term at the state's Yuma prison complex in San Luis. Scott Smith appears to have served his time and been released.

As for the deadly daughter-in-law, Doris Ann Carlson is incarcerated for life at the Arizona Department of Corrections prison complex in the town of Goodyear. Gone is the youthful, pudgy face and glasses. Now her hair is short and she looks thin, worn and soulless.

The Football Booster

NO ONE CAN SAY CHERISH ARROYO DIDN'T GIVE HER all for the Copper Canyon High School football team.

Problem is, the Litchfield Park, Arizona woman gave *too much* of herself to members of the squad, the same one her teenage son played on.

The thirty-five year old wife and mother of two was treasurer of the team's booster club, a group of parents who raise money so the team can buy uniforms, travel and play other teams, and take part in wholesome activities that build team spirit.

After she was arrested September 20, 2011 she confessed to having sex with two of her son's teammates. She hinted that she had scored with even more.

Copper Canyon High School is in a rural area outside of Glendale, Arizona, just west of Phoenix. It's named for a series of canyons to the southwest, in Mexico, which is larger and deeper than the state's own Grand Canyon. The four-year high school has about 1,700 students. The athletic teams are called the Aztecs—the logo is the head of a warrior—and the school colors are a busy black, teal, copper and purple.

The school was completed in 2005 and is more than a quarter-million square feet. In addition to a state-of-the art performing arts center, there's a football field designed by an architectural firm famous for building professional ballparks, stadiums and training facilities.

Like other towns big and small across America, high school football is king.

The school's mission statement is "Aztecs Aspire, Aztecs Achieve." Eighty-nine percent of the students are Hispanic, and many come from low-income families.

By all appearances, Cherish Arroyo, her husband, and their two sons were doing better than most of the parents whose children attended Copper Canyon High School. They lived in Litchfield Park in a newer, tan, two-story home with a Spanish-tile roof and two cars in the drive-way, a truck and a VW Bora. The Bora had numerous stickers on the back championing Cherish's favorite team, the Aztecs.

But Cherish wasn't feeling very *cherished*. She was lonely, and fed up with her husband watching up to ten hours of college football every Saturday. She spent a lot of her time on Facebook. She described being on-line as being in a "trance."

Which got her into trouble.

She started to flirt with boys on the football team. She invited them over for dinner. And then she left suggestive messages on the Facebook page of one seventeen-year old.

His parents discovered it accidentally one day. When they asked him about the messages he admitted to having both oral sex and intercourse with Arroyo on three separate occasions when he was 16. Their rendezvous, he said, took place in the home Cherish shared with her children and husband.

The parents contacted the Maricopa County Sheriff's Office.

Sheriff Joe Arpaio set up a phone call between the boy and Cherish to see if she would implicate herself. She did. During the call, the boy told her that his parents saw the Facebook messages and believed they were having sex. She responded by stating that she could be sent to jail since he was a minor.

She was taken to the sheriff's office and interviewed. She admitted having sex with the boy "multiple times."

The sheriff didn't go into detail about what the Facebook messages said, but did describe one."It was something like, 'I have some medicine for you," Arpaio said.

When Arroyo was booked on six counts of sexual conduct with a minor she admitted having sex with a second boy. The sheriff issued a statement saying other possible victims should come forward. He believed there were at least a few more football players out there who the mom had befriended.

Cherish Arroyo spent a night in jail, and was released on $9,000 bond. And then she went home to the tan two-story house with the car and pickup in the driveway, wearing an electronic monitoring device until her preliminary court hearing.

The community was shocked by the arrest of the treasurer of the Aztec's booster club. One male student seemed to identify with the embarrassment she caused her children. He told a local television station, "Their mom should be supporting them, not...doing something else."

One mother, about the same age as Arroyo, commented, "It kind of doesn't make you feel safe to have your students out here going to school."

JOE ARPAIO CALLS HIMSELF "AMERICA'S TOUGHEST sheriff." He is also one of the most-investigated.

Since 2008, his office—the largest sheriff's department in Arizona—has been investigated by the Justice Department and the FBI time and again, for civil rights violations, abuse of power, substandard jail conditions, and a long list of other allegations.

Among his most controversial acts: bringing back chain gangs (for women and juveniles, too); saving money by feeding convicts just two meals a day; and making males wear pink boxers.

Nevertheless, Sheriff Arpaio, first elected in 1992, continues to be re-elected. His self-published autobiography is titled *Joe's Law: America's Toughest Sheriff Takes on Illegal Immigration, Drugs and Everything Else That Threatens America.*

The *Everything Else That Threatens America* includes women who are a menace to Arpaio's world. Maricopa County seems to have more than its share of women committing serious crimes.

Cherish Arroyo's story bears a resemblance to the case of Susan Brock, a case that rocked the county in the same year, 2011. Brock, the devoutly Mormon mother of three and wife of a Maricopa County Supervisor, is serving a 13-year prison sentence for sexually abusing a teenage friend of the family for three years, starting in 2006 when the boy was 13. Her then 18-year old daughter, Rachel, received ten years' probation for sexually abusing the same boy.

In February, 2014 German-born Debra Milke, who had been sentenced to death for conspiring to have her four-year-old son murdered, was released from the Maricopa County jail. After spending more than two decades on death row, her conviction was overturned by the 9th U.S. Circuit Court of Appeals, which threw out a confession she said she never made which was not recorded. She was freed but is scheduled to be retried.

CHERISH ARROYO ISN'T THE FIRST MOM TO GET inappropriately involved with children. Female teachers have made most of the news about crossing the line. Cherish has more than a few traits in common with the wave of female teachers who have been arrested in recent years for having sex with their students.

Like MaryKay LeTourneau, Pamela Smart, Debra Lafave, Jennifer Leigh Rice and the dozens of others who have been caught, 35-year old Cherish is pretty and looks young for her age. She has dark, shoulder length hair and a round face. She could pass for her early twenties, rather than her mid-thirties. But there is an immaturity that goes with her youthful face. She friended the boys on Facebook. She began flirting with them because she was lonely and neglected by her husband. Rather than find a mature way to cope with the ups and downs in her marriage, she behaved as if she were a peer of the boys—not their friend's mother.

While there's a double standard for female sex offenders—they get lighter sentences than male pedophiles, and society sees it as boys getting "lucky" when they are sexually initiated by an experienced woman—the ramifications for boys are just as damaging as they are for girls who are victims. Studies on CSA (childhood sexual abuse) indicate that boys who are abused by women are twice as likely to attempt suicide; are more likely to marry an alcoholic and report marital problems; are more apt to be involved with the criminal justice system; and are at a higher risk for future abuse and exploitation as an adult.

CHERISH ARROYO HAD ONE PRINCIPAL DEFENSE: SHE blamed her narcolepsy medication.

She had been diagnosed with narcolepsy—a neurological sleep disorder characterized by excessive daytime sleepiness and sudden bouts of sleep that can strike at any time—in 2009, two years before she had sex with the student. She said she took the medication to regulate her sleep cycles and that it could induce sleep in as little as fifteen minutes.

According to Arroyo, each of the sexual encounters occurred while she was under the influence of the medication, and as a result she was not conscious of her actions. In essence, she was saying the boy took advantage of her while she was in a drug-induced sleep.

However, she was awake, she admitted, during Facebook conversations.

Her physician testified that the drug she took is related to another drug which can cause sleepwalking. Cherish's husband testified that the medication sometimes made her act "differently." He explained that if she is under the influence, "whoever wakes her up is basically in control of her." He gave as examples times he had found her eating, drinking, checking their son's blood sugar, and even doing housework while asleep.

The jury found Arroyo guilty of five of six counts of sexual conduct with a minor and sentenced her to lifetime probation plus nine months' jail time. The Arizona Court of Appeals found no grounds for her appeal. She had, after all, admitted having sex with a minor, and said during the recorded phone call that she feared going to jail because he was a minor.

No other cases were brought against Cherish, probably because other boys she had sex with were over age eighteen, the age of consent in Arizona.

Cherish Arroyo is required to register as a sex offender in Arizona, but she doesn't appear on the sex offender registry. That may mean that she is considered a level 1 sex offender (low risk). Arizona is not required to make those public.

No one knows if she still lives with her husband and two sons. In December, 2013 her appeal was overturned. A copy of it was mailed to her. It was returned to the court as undeliverable.

Afterword

TO LEARN MORE ABOUT FEMALE TEACHERS WHO have inappropriate relationships with underage students, read *Bad Apples—Inside the Teacher/Student Sex Scandal Epidemic,* by Rebecca Morris. It's the first book to look specifically at why female teachers, coaches and even school board members risk everything to have sex with students. It also examines gender bias in sentencing, the psychological effect on the children who are molested, the role of social networking and the media, and how parents and schools can keep students safe. Available on Kindle and Nook.

PHOTO ARCHIVE

The Fourth Wife Photos

Deborah Delaney had always been attracted to firefighters. But Bill Delaney told a lot of lies about himself and his career.

Bill Delaney worked fast. He was dating just days after his third wife died mysteriously.

Freed—But Are They Innocent?
Photos

Joyce Sterrenberg and Timothy McKillop worked together at Mountain Bell Telephone and were planning a life together.

The two 20-year olds were found murdered on a dirt road east of Scottsdale on May 24, 1962. They had recently told their families they planned to marry.

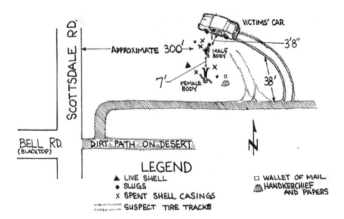

A police sketch of the crime scene. Twelve years would pass before there was an arrest.

In 1974, Bill Macumber's estranged wife said he had confessed to the murders. He was convicted two years later. Macumber's attorneys believe his wife, who worked at the sheriff's office, tampered with evidence.

Bill Macumber shortly before he was released in 2012. As part of a deal he entered a plea of no contest to the murders.

Debra Milke and her son Christopher. On the day he disappeared, December 2, 1989, he thought he was going to the mall to see Santa Claus.

Despite his mother's struggles to make a life for the two of them, in photographs Christopher always looked happy.

Milke was convicted of hiring two men to kill her son and became the first woman sentenced to death in Arizona in sixty years.

James Styers and his friend Roger Scott. They pointed the finger at each other.

Debra Milke was convicted in part because of the controversial testimony of Detective Armando Saldate, Jr.

The dry river bed in the Arizona desert where little Christopher's body was found.

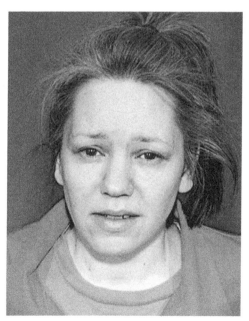

Debra Milke at the time of her release in 2013. She could be re-tried.

The Vicious Vixen Photos

*Jodi Arias, as a blonde, and Travis Alexander in happier times.
There weren't many of them.*

*Jodi Arias answering questions from the jury via the judge in
her murder trial.*

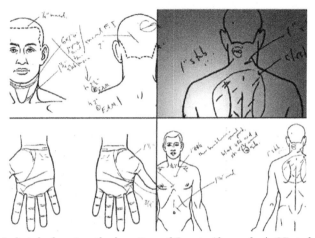

*A sketch showing the location of Travis Alexander's 27 stab
wounds and bullet to the head.*

The Deadly Daughter-in-Law
Photos

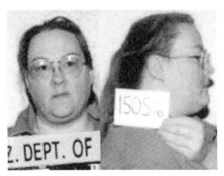

Doris Ann Carlson was a mother-in-law's worst nightmare.

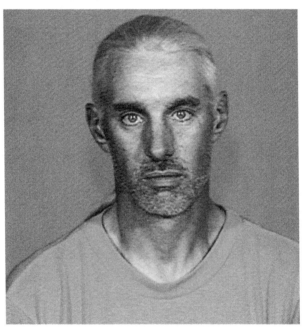

David Carlson stood to inherit from his mother but he and his wife got greedy.

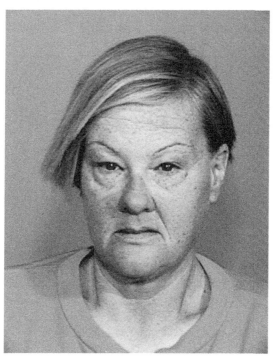

In 2002 Doris Ann Carlson's sentence was changed from death to life in prison.

The Football Booster Photos

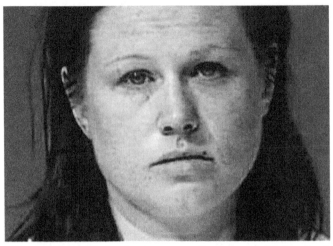

Cherish Arroyo helped raise money for her son's high school football team. She confessed to having sex with two of the athletes—and may have scored with even more.

FUNDAMENTAL LOVE

GREGG OLSEN
AND
REBECCA MORRIS

NOTORIOUS
UTAH

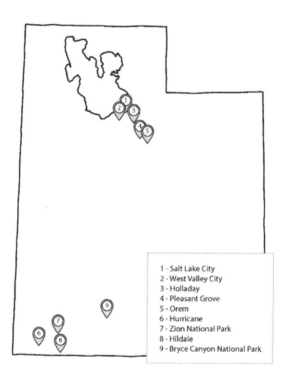

1 - Salt Lake City
2 - West Valley City
3 - Holladay
4 - Pleasant Grove
5 - Orem
6 - Hurricane
7 - Zion National Park
8 - Hildale
9 - Bryce Canyon National Park

Baby Killer

ON A SPRING DAY IN 2014, DARREN WEST WAS tackling the garage. Doing some cleaning and sorting was a step in starting over.

He had worked in construction before being sent to federal prison in 2006 for possessing the chemicals that compose methamphetamine (he said he was carrying the package for a friend). He had an earlier offense, too—in 1991 when he was 18 he had pleaded guilty to raping a 13 year old.

Now Darren West was 41, just out of prison and living at a half-way house. Estranged from his wife, Megan Huntsman, he wanted to eventually move back into the house with their three daughters, two teenagers and a 20-year old. The two-family rambler in Pleasant Grove, Utah, was owned by his parents. Megan and their daughters had lived in the house while he was in prison. But his parents had one condition to her staying in the house—that she was faithful to their son. She hadn't been, so they had asked her to leave. She had moved into her boyfriend's trailer, leaving her three daughters with Darren's relatives. She had recently lost her job at a supermarket bakery.

On Saturday, April 12, 2014 he was permitted to leave the half-way house to get some of his belongings. As he sorted through the garage, he opened some boxes to see if they were items to keep or to toss. He reached for one that sat near an artificial Christmas tree and a bag of old shoes. It was sealed with electrical tape and labeled "Baby stuff—Megan's." He wondered what it was. Their three daughters were nearly grown. Maybe it was time to throw or give away baby items. As he opened it he was overcome by a foul smell. Unwrapping the contents he found an infant, dead for some time, wrapped in plastic and a blanket. It was just the first of seven tiny bodies police would find.

THERE ARE MANY CRIMES THAT ARE SHOCKING. THE most shocking is mothers who kill their children.

"Maternal filicide" is the killing of a child by its mother; "infanticide" is the intentional killing of a child under 12 months of age; and "neonaticide" is killing a child within 24 hours of birth.

Megan Huntsman fit the criteria for all three.

Although men are more likely to kill children, hundreds of women in the U.S. kill their children every year—because of mental illness, neglect, greed, selfishness, by accident, or because they were impaired at the time.

Robin Row (see "Notorious Idaho") killed her three children in two separate fires to collect life insurance on them. Diane Downs ("Notorious Oregon") shot her three children, killing one and seriously injuring the other two, so she would be free to pursue a relationship with a married man. Angela McAnulty ("Notorious Oregon") tortured her teenage daughter to death. Tanya Reid ("Notorious Texas") was responsible for the death of her baby daughter and nearly killed her son before it was determined that she had Munchausen Syndrome by Proxy. In MSBP a parent makes a child appear sick or actually causes harm to the child in order to get attention themselves.

There have been young women—usually teenagers who are isolated, have no support, and are unmarried—who keep an unwanted pregnancy secret and dispose of an infant at birth.

The rare case that elicited sympathy was that of Andrea Yates, who drowned her five children in a bathtub. She suffered a psychological breakdown and suffered from extreme postpartum psychosis.

The only one on the same scale as Megan Huntsman's is the case of a French woman who gave birth to eight babies over 17 years and buried them in a garden. She told police that she didn't want any more children but didn't want to see a doctor for birth control.

A psychiatrist for another French woman who hid three newborns in a deep freezer said she suffered from a condition called "pregnancy denial."

It's too early still to understand why and how Megan Huntsman concealed seven pregnancies from her husband, children, family and neighbors, giving birth seven times without anyone knowing.

LIFE WAS NOT EASY FOR MEGAN HUNTSMAN. HER alcohol and drug used contributed to her poor decision-making. When she was young her mother had been ill with cancer. Her father, who suffered from chronic pain, committed suicide. She met Darren West in high school and by 18 she was married. The couple fell into using—and possibly attempting to make—methamphetamine.

Pleasant Grove is a conservative community of about 35,000 about 35 miles south of Salt Lake City. The town has one tavern and 12 churches. Megan was raised Mormon, but no longer attended church.

Some neighbors described her as "a nice, quiet woman," and "a great babysitter" who often helped care for their children and baked cookies for them. "She loved kids," one of them told a local newspaper. Others thought she was cold and hard to get to know. While Darren worked construction, Megan babysat or cleaned houses to make extra money.

Some neighbors had noticed that her weight fluctuated over the years. She was 5'4" and weighed only 105 pounds, but she never seemed pregnant, and never told anyone that she was.

THE FIRST THING DARREN WEST DID WHEN HE found the dead infant was call his estranged wife at her boyfriend's trailer.

She admitted she had given birth to the baby. Then he called the police. They searched the garage and found six more tiny babies in boxes. She was arrested the next day.

In her interviews with police she said she had literally lost count of the number of times she had been pregnant. They wanted to know how many bodies they should look for. She gave police a "ballpark" number, telling them she thought there were eight or nine infants in the garage. There were seven—six she had killed and one was stillborn.

Detectives described her as acting "perfectly normal" as she talked about the pregnancies.

During those years she hadn't seemed worried about the amount of drugs she took and alcohol she consumed. She was often "high." She gave little or no thought to whether her babies might be born with complications.

Law enforcement had missed an earlier opportunity to find the babies. In 2005 when they were investigating Darren West on drug charges Megan permitted them to search the home and even the garage. Two weeks after he was indicted, Utah's Division of Child and Human Services received a tip that Megan was using methamphetamine. It's not clear if or how the agency responded.

For months after discovering the seven infants in the boxes, police implied Megan Huntsman had a motive and she had acted on it. It was *not* a case of mental illness, they said, that drove her to kill and hide the babies. Finally they explained that during an interview, she had told detectives that she needed money to buy drugs and felt she needed to choose between babies and drugs. She didn't want the babies or the responsibility that came with them.

Defense attorneys around the country weighed in on cable TV—how could it be anything BUT mental illness? Maybe one is an accident, but seven?

Darren West said he had not known about the seven pregnancies (all were before he went to prison in 2006), and in fact, he'd been unaware that Megan had been pregnant until the moment she delivered their first two children, the girls who are now-teenagers. He has not been charged with helping conceal the seven tiny bodies.

Megan had never seen a doctor during her 10 pregnancies. She gave birth to all of her children, including her three living ones, in the house.

After moving in with her boyfriend, Megan got pregnant again, and miscarried. Her boyfriend said he was unaware of it. On the day they arrested her at the trailer, they found Xanax, marijuana and bongs.

An inactive Facebook page has a photo of three pretty girls, presumably her daughters.

DNA TESTS ON THE INFANTS FINALLY GAVE THE police and community some answers.

All seven infants were born full term.

There were five girls and two boys.

Darren West was the biological father of all seven.

Megan Huntsman either choked or smothered each baby immediately after birth.

Decay was so extensive it could not be determined when each child was born or when it died.

MEGAN HUNTSMAN MIGHT HAVE FACED THE DEATH PENALTY. She won't because the babies were killed before 2006. Until 2007, killing a child was not considered one of the aggravating factors that makes someone eligible for the death penalty in Utah.

If convicted she faces five years to life on each of the seven murder counts.

She is being held on six million dollars bail—one million for each baby she strangled and smothered. Her friends and neighbors are still shocked at the news that the woman they described as "a nice, quiet woman," and "a great babysitter" who often helped care for their own children and baked them cookies, is capable of killing infants, boxing them up, and leaving them in a garage.

Afterword

ACCORDING TO SEARCH WARRANTS, THESE ARE details of the seven newborns:

Baby number one was wrapped in plastic bags and a green towel and stuffed into a white box that had been sealed with electrical tape.

Baby number two was wrapped in garbage bags and towels and in a box.

Baby number three was covered in plastic and stuffed into a shoe box wrapped in a blue sweatshirt then held shut with electrical tape.

Baby number four was found under two blankets and two bath towels in the bottom left corner of a cubby.

Baby number five was laid to rest inside a cabinet on the east wall of the garage among a white apple box, a green hand towel and a red and green blanket.

Baby number six was wrapped in a sweater and hidden in a cabinet that held diapers, plastic wrap and a T-shirt emblazoned with the Budweiser logo.

Baby number seven was covered with pink and brown towels and placed in a large box inside a black garbage bag.

Police also seized letters, documents, a tablet device, bloody leather gloves, and furniture, including a mattress, belonging to Megan Huntsman and some items she stored at her mother's.

Deadly Distraction

LIKE MANY PARENTS, MORNINGS WERE THE BUSIEST time for 32-year old April Suwyn. She saw her husband, Micah, off to work. She dropped her daughter, Skyah, at a neighbor's house. She took her two young sons to daycare. Then there was her job—she was a manicurist and had a salon in her house.

Life was busy, but the pretty woman with nearly waist-length brown hair doted on her family. Photographs show the proud parents with their two young sons, one blonde and one dark haired, and Skyah—about to celebrate her first birthday—with a pink ribbon in her hair. The girl had dimples, big blue eyes, and an even bigger grin.

August 1, 2014 was a normal morning for April and her children, until she decided to break routine and keep Skyah in the car while she dropped her sons at daycare.

That's when April realized she needed a bathroom, badly. She could stop at the gym, or a fast food restaurant, but she decided to rush home. Nearing her neighborhood in Hurricane, Utah—just across the border from Nevada—April groaned as she saw yet another obstacle to her morning. There was construction blocking her street in their rural neighborhood.

Could anything else go wrong?

She parked several blocks away and made a run for it.

Now she could take a deep breath—she was home and could get a start on the rest of her day.

Several hours later, April went into the nursery to get Skyah up from her regular morning nap. It was time to pick up the boys from daycare.

The crib was empty.

The temperature in Hurricane that day rose to 100 degrees. It was even hotter in the car, where little Skyah had been left for several hours.

Paramedics were called and Skyah was airlifted to Dixie Regional Medical Center. She was pronounced dead on arrival.

April can't forgive herself, her family is in deep grief, and she faced criminal charges in the death of her child.

JUST A FEW WEEKS BEFORE SKYAH DIED, AN Arizona father stood trial for the death of his three-month old son in a car.

Thirty-three year old Daniel Bryant Gray was arrested after his son Jamison was found unresponsive in his car parked outside the bar where Gray worked. The child was in the car for nearly three hours before Gray remembered him.

He ran to the car, picked up the baby, and took him inside the bar. He plunged him into a cooler of ice, screaming and trying to bring the boy back to life. But Jamison was dead.

Gray smoked marijuana with coworkers while the boy baked in the car. A judge said she did not believe that the use of the drug was *why* he forgot the boy in the car.

Prosecutors decided that while the death was unintentional, Gray had a responsibility to know his son's whereabouts.

WHO LEAVES A CHILD TO DIE IN A HOT CAR? PARENTS do—the good ones and the negligent ones.

But when is it an accident, and when is it murder?

Around forty children die every year after they're forgotten in a car, something that seems inconceivable to most adults. But the summer of 2014 shocked people who thought they had heard it all.

Thirty-three year old Justin Ross Harris—known as 'Ross'—and his wife of eight years, Leanna, are conservative Christians. In Internet postings, Ross Harris wrote about his views on abortion and why he favors teaching creationism in schools. He had other, on-line habits that he tried to keep secret.

After a short career in law enforcement, Ross finished college and worked as a web developer.

On June 18, 2014, Harris took his son, 22-month old Cooper, to a Chik-fil-A restaurant for breakfast. Then he buckled the boy into his car seat in the 2011 Hyundai—on what police described as the lowest and tightest setting possible—and drove to his job at the corporate headquarters of Home Depot outside Atlanta, Ga. He parked his SUV in a company parking lot and went to work.

Normally, he would drop Cooper at daycare. He didn't that day. Left in the hot car for several hours, the boy clawed at his face and had abrasions on the back of his head from his attempts to get free.

And what was Ross Harris doing as his son struggled and died? Police say he was exchanging nude photos with six women—including a teenage girl. He even returned to the parking lot midday to put some packages in the car.

Seven hours after he arrived at work, Harris left and drove for several minutes before supposedly "finding" the boy's dead body.

Police wonder why he didn't smell it. Hours later, after a stranger called the police, the smell still permeated the car.

Detectives said Ross and Leanna seemed unemotional after learning their son died. Employees at the day care center said that when Leanna went to pick up her son and was told her husband hadn't dropped off Cooper that morning, Leanna responded, "Ross must have left him in the car." During police questioning, Leanna reportedly asked her husband, "Did you say too much?" In the weeks before Cooper's death, Ross Harris had searched the Internet for articles and videos on life without children, on the painful death of animals left in hot cars, and even how to survive in prison.

In bringing criminal charges, the prosecutor said the sexting "goes to the state of mind" of the defendant. The Harris' were having marital problems and Harris "wanted a child free life," the prosecutor said.

And then there's the life insurance. The couple had two insurance policies on their son, one worth $2,000 through Harris' employer and a second policy worth $25,000 the couple took out in November 2012.

Harris was charged with murder and child cruelty. When he appeared in court to plead not guilty, his wife looked on, chewing gum and seeming disinterested.

Prosecutors are still investigating her possible role in the child's death. They say she also researched hot car deaths online. What they haven't said is *when* the couple did their research. If it was weeks or months before Cooper's death it could mean they had read about another child's death and wanted to prevent such an incident. Cases had been in the news. If it was hours or days before the boy's death, it would be more suspicious.

It's called "death by hyperthermia" and it is not an easy death. Children literally bake to death as the interiors of cars reach a temperature of up to 140 degrees. Death occurs when the core body temperature warms and reaches 108 degrees. But heatstroke can happen even on a day that isn't hot. The interior of a car can reach well over 110 degrees even when the outside temperature is in the 60s.

More than 600 children have died of hyperthermia in cars in the U.S. since 1998. Families are broken, parents feel guilt and are suicidal, and sometimes an incarcerated parent is separated from their other children.

Some of the deaths are clearly accidents. Experts say that in about 40 percent of cases a car death is accidental, usually a mistake of memory. In the other 60 percent of the cases, authorities decide that the negligence was so great that it must be handled as a felony. The organization KidsAndCars.org said 81 percent of criminal charges resulted in convictions or guilty pleas and half the people went to jail for a median sentence of two years.

In his 2009 Pulitzer Prize-winning magazine article in The Washington Post, Gene Weingarten kept his focus on child hyperthermia cases that were pure accidents, avoiding any cases involving abuse or neglect. He could empathize with the parents he interviewed, admitting that he nearly left his own young daughter in a car in Miami one hot day. He wrote that she would have been trapped in the car if she hadn't woken from a nap just as he was climbing out.

He set out to learn why even good parents sometimes leave a child in a car to die.

Our brains are to blame. People forget children in their cars because of four key reasons: stress, emotional reasons, lack of sleep, and—most importantly—a change in routine. Our memory circuits become confused.

One of many sad cases that illustrates the deadly combination of a change in routine and fatigue is the death of a 9-month old boy in a hot car in Santa Clara, Ca. in July, 2014. The mother normally took two older children to school and dropped the baby off at a babysitter. But she had started a new job the night before and her husband was watching the children at night. On the day the baby died, the father—with only four hours sleep—forgot about the change in the family's routine. He took the older children to school, then left his car and picked up the vending machine delivery truck he drove, forgetting that the baby was in a car seat in the back of the car. The father didn't discover his mistake until he returned to his car that evening.

The Santa Clara County District Attorney's Office considered filing involuntary manslaughter and child endangerment charges against the man, but would have had to prove beyond a reasonable doubt that he was negligent or reckless. Authorities decided not to bring criminal charges, calling the death "a tragic mistake" and said fatigue was to blame.

The New York Daily News felt compelled to point out in its headline that a man in Kansas who is accused of leaving a 10-month-old baby in a car on a 90-degree day. Twenty-nine year old Seth Jackson has been charged with first degree murder in the girl's death and can have no contact with his husband or the five other adopted and foster children they have. He was watching television with another child at the time and forgot about the girl in the car. He faces 15 years in prison—more time than a drunk driver who killed someone would serve.

A 15-month-old New York state girl died after spending hours locked in a vehicle that her father had parked outside her grandparents' house. The baby's father brought one child to a family member's home, dropped two more off at school and drove to the grandfather's house with the baby. He switched to a different car and drove to work, leaving the infant behind. Police deemed it an accident.

But not all cases of child hyperthermia in cars are caused by memory lapses. In some cases there is a history of prior neglect or evidence of substance abuse. Sometimes parents knowingly take a chance, choosing to leave a child in a car. One woman used her locked car as an inexpensive substitute for day care. Another left her child while she went for a job interview. Two children in Houston were rescued as their mother shopped. In a near-miss, a two-month old girl was found in a minivan; her mother had left her while she took another child to a pediatrician appointment.

Only twenty states, including Utah, have laws specifically addressing a child left unattended in a car. They vary regarding the age of the child and length of time they are left in the car, and some only apply when the conditions represent a significant threat to the child, or result in injury or death.

The laws seem not so different than those addressing pets. In fourteen states it's illegal to leave an animal in a confined car.

THERE IS NO COURT LIKE THE COURT OF PUBLIC opinion. Whenever a child dies in a car—whether by accident, negligence, or homicide—parents are demonized on-line.

After Skyah Suwyn died in Hurricane, Utah, thousands of people took to social media to offer sympathy and even money to the family. Others were outraged. For a time there were dueling Facebook pages—one supporting April Suwyn, the other calling for her arrest.

Most of the comments posted on the New York Daily News website debated whether or not the paper went too far in pointing out that the foster father in Kansas was gay.

Gene Weingarten, the Washington Post writer, said of the hatred expressed on social media, "We need to believe these parents are monsters because it's too uncomfortable for most of us to acknowledge that it could happen to us."

He said he had hoped his 2009 Washington Post story would help lower the death rate of children left in hot cars. It hasn't.

If it seems we hear more about hot car deaths than we used to, there's a good reason. In the 1990s, car-safety experts recommended that child seats be moved to the back of the car because of the danger of airbags. Then it was decided that baby seats should face the rear. Small children in the car were suddenly less visible to drivers.

For years, groups have lobbied for a law requiring backseat sensors in new cars. Supporters say an auto manufacturers' lobby has blocked the bill. A few entrepreneurs have come up with ideas to prevent hot car deaths. After a colleague accidentally left his 9-month-old son to die in a parking lot in Hampton, VA, three NASA engineers patented a device with weight sensors and a keychain alarm. They've never found a manufacturer.

Even children have come up with ideas. A boy in Tennessee invented what he calls the EZ Baby Saver. It's a large rubber band attached to the car door that reminds the driver that a child is in the car. There's another, simple, idea that has been shared on the Internet: after buckling a child into a car seat, a driver takes off his or her left shoe and puts it on the back seat. Once they reach their destination, they won't go far without the shoe, and they'll be reminded of the child.

IN LATE AUGUST, 2014 PROSECUTORS IN UTAH SAID they would not seek criminal charges against April Suwyn.

They said charging her for her 11-month old daughter's death is "not in the interest of justice," and that the death of little Skyah was caused by "a lack of sleep, changed routine, and stress."

On September 4, 2014 a Cobb County, Georgia grand jury indicted Justin Ross Harris on multiple charges including malice murder, felony murder, and cruelty to children for his son's death. He plead not guilty. Prosecutors say they will not seek the death penalty. His wife, Leanna, has not been arrested.

Daniel Bryant Gray was sentenced to four years in prison in Arizona for leaving his three-month old son to die.

And children continue to die in cars.

The Lego Murder

TWO WOMEN, BOTH LOYAL AND HARDWORKING members of their respective faiths, both murdered by the people they were trying to help.

Cold cases—when solved—are solved in the strangest ways. A small plastic toy with a fingerprint may be one of the strangest.

Lucille Johnson was active, in good health, and a devout member of the Church of Jesus Christ of Latter-day Saints. A widow, she lived alone in her Holladay, Utah home, a large brown house at the top of a hilly driveway in the Salt Lake City suburb. The front of the house had metal decorative railings and awnings to keep out a little of the bright sun.

She was a good person and a good friend. She had recently visited a neighbor who was in the hospital and brought food to another who was ill. Her grown children, Jerry and Shirley, kept a loving eye on their 78-year old mother.

The last time Lucille Johnson was seen alive, February 1, 1991, she was sweeping the porch of her house. The next day her daughter found her beaten and strangled. A few pieces of jewelry were missing.

Police couldn't help but notice Lego building blocks scattered on the living room floor, in the entry way to the house, and even on the driveway. Johnson's children said she did have toys for her grandchildren, but she would never leave them lying around.

Her daughter described Lucille Johnson as "very tender, very dear" and an energetic woman with many years ahead of her. Where had the Legos come from? Had there been a child nearby when this exceptional woman was murdered?

FORTY-ONE YEAR OLD ELIZABETH CALABRESE— Trudy to her friends—was an active member of her church, Living Springs Assembly of God in Glendale, Arizona. She had retired after a 20-year career in the military as a medical technician. She liked volunteering because it allowed her to demonstrate her religious beliefs.

On a cold, rainy day, February 24, 1998, the mother of two was delivering emergency food boxes to families that needed help. One of the calls that day was from a family with four young children. The caller explained that he and his wife had just gotten jobs and they were waiting for paychecks to buy food. Volunteers were usually required to work in pairs but that day Calabrese decided to make the trip alone. She didn't want the children to go hungry. Her fellow-volunteers said she was smiling as she left with two boxes of groceries.

She didn't return.

The caller was 31-year old John Sansing. He did have four children and they needed groceries—but what he really needed was money to buy crack cocaine. He called his wife several times at work that day to talk about how to get more crack. He said he had had some and had smoked it, but saved a little for her.

His wife, Kara, 28, returned home at 3:20 p.m. and the couple smoked what crack was left. In front of their four children he said he planned to rob the person who delivered the food.

Sansing had married Kara, also known as Nomi Lamphere, after meeting her at a mall. She had run away from an abusive home in Bangladesh and wound up in a Calcutta jail. Her luck could have changed when she was adopted by a Salt Lake City social worker, Ann Lamphere. But Kara hadn't been able to escape the dysfunction she'd known all her life. She married John Sansing, a thief and drug addict who beat her.

"In the East Indian culture, the husband is the one in charge, who is always right and can even tell the wife to kill herself," her adopted mother, Lamphere, told the Arizona Republic. "She was definitely of that culture. She wouldn't leave him despite all the abuse." He worked as a warehouse stocker and they had four children in the first few years of marriage.

A landlord said the family often sought help from charitable organizations and that the children were encouraged to scrounge for handouts, including cigarette money for their father.

Trudy arrived at the house at 4 p.m. with two boxes of food. As John wrote out a receipt, she and Kara chatted in the kitchen. Suddenly, he grabbed Trudy from behind. In front of their children, the couple tied Trudy up with electrical cords. According to court documents, she prayed as she was being bound, saying "Lord, please help me" and "I don't want to die, but if this is the way you want me to come home, I am ready." She begged the children to call 911. John Sansing struck her hard enough in the head that he broke the club he used.

He told the children to go into the living room and watch TV.

Leaving her on the dining room floor, Sansing took her keys and moved her truck, then returned to the house and dragged her into a bedroom. She had regained consciousness and he stuffed a sock in her mouth and put two plastic bags over her head and secured them with cords and a necktie. Then he raped her and stabbed her three times in the abdomen, deliberately twisting the knife inside her. According to the medical examiner, she lived several minutes more. His wife watched it all.

Sansing removed Trudy's jewelry and left the body in the bedroom, covered with clothing, for several hours. He did two drug deals immediately after the murder—trading Trudy's rings for crack cocaine, and then her necklace for more.

Later that evening the pastor of Trudy's church called looking for her. Sansing gave a fake address and said she had never arrived.

The couple went to sleep in the living room. In the middle of the night he got up and hid her body under cardboard boxes between a shed and a wall in the back yard. At least three of the children saw the body in the yard. Sansing washed the bloody club and hid the clothing he had covered her with after killing her.

That evening, the search for Trudy Calabrese began when her husband, a retired Air Force officer, reported her missing. Her truck was found the next day, along with a piece of paper with the Sansing's correct address. Sansing confided to his sister that he had murdered the woman delivering food boxes; she told their father, and he called the police.

When detectives arrived they found a filthy home. The carpet was littered with garbage and dog feces. They found a knife under a sofa cushion, the wooden club under a sink, and Trudy's body behind the shed. They arrested John Sansing. Because of his long history of felony convictions in Utah he was held without bond. They also arrested his wife, Kara, and set her bond at $500,000.

Their four children - three boys ages 10, 11, and 12 and a 9-year-old girl—were placed in the care of Sansing's sister.

During John Sansing's trial, his defense presented what they hoped were mitigating factors, claiming drug use, a difficult childhood, a lack of education, and the fact he expressed remorse and accepted responsibility for the crime. Of course, his acceptance of responsibility didn't include *other* crimes he knew he had committed. On appeal, the court said there was no link between Sansing's childhood and the horrific crime.

JOHN SANSING PLEAD GUILTY AND WAS SENTENCED to death in 1999. His death sentence was upheld in 2003. His attorneys continue to appeal to the courts, most recently in 2013, hoping to stay his execution.

Kara Sansing testified against her husband as part of a plea deal. Between sobs, she recounted every grisly detail of the murder - and Calabrese's final prayer. She was sentenced to life in prison, avoiding the death penalty.

A chilling video of police interviewing their children was played in court. The interviews were taped the day after the murder. The three oldest children speak matter-of-factly about watching their parents attack Trudy Calabrese.

The 9-year old girl relates how her daddy killed the "church lady" who came to their home to bring them free food. "He grabbed her from behind. .. he tied her up," she said. The children said they listened as Calabrese prayed. She had also pleaded with the children three or four times to call the police and 911. Instead, they obeyed their parents' orders to go watch cartoons.

One of the boys talked of seeing Trudy's tears, and of hearing his father threaten to hit her if she didn't stop moving. He remembered hearing the blow to the back of her skull. He saw the blood on her head, and her body after it was moved to the backyard shed.

"They wanted money," he said of his parents.

"Did she have any money?" the police officer asked.

"She had some change," the boy said. "A dollar twenty-five."

During his sentencing, Judge Ronald S. Reinstein called Elizabeth Calabrese a "good Samaritan" and a person who "took great joy in helping people in need," keeping her faith in God to the end. In the appeal of his death sentence, Sansing's lawyers claimed the judge based his sentence on the victim's good character, essentially imposing the death sentence because he viewed the victim as a person above the norm of other murder victims. The appeals court did not agree. It also found the crime "senseless," because Sansing did not need to kill Calabrese in order to rob her. This murder, the court wrote, was especially cruel. This was not a "robbery gone bad"—this was a murder committed for the purpose of robbery.

Elizabeth Calabrese's husband, Rosario Calabrese, said he cannot hate the people charged with brutalizing and killing his wife.

"I believe they are on drugs and don't know what they are doing," he said. "I know they have to pay the price before God, but I don't know what to feel."

He was told by the other volunteers that his wife was smiling when she set out on the delivery. "She was always smiling and trying to do God's work, and that is how I think she would want us to remember her," he said.

TWENTY-THREE YEARS AFTER LUCILLE JOHNSON was murdered, and 16 years after he was sent to Arizona's death row for the murder of Trudy Calabrese, two Utah detectives reopened Johnson's murder.

DNA testing wasn't available in 1991, but investigators sent scrapings that had been collected and saved from under Johnson's fingernails for testing and got a match—to now- 47-year old John Sansing. They then matched the fingerprints on the red, yellow, and black plastic Lego squares to Sansing's son, five years old at the time. The boy had played with his Legos while his father killed the elderly widow in her bed. The Legos must have been scattered as father and son quickly left the house.

They interviewed the son, now an adult, who recalled being with his dad. According to Sheriff Jim Winder, the little boy had witnessed *two* murders, Lucille Johnson and Trudy Calabrese. "It becomes even more tragic for this man," says the sheriff. "That young child has been tormented by these visions all these years."

Sansing may have taken the child along to appear non-threatening to a woman answering the door.

Kara Sansing has admitted she knew her husband had murdered a woman in Utah. A nephew said he twice heard Kara threaten Sansing that she would tell the police about the earlier murder.

At a news conference announcing the solving of Johnson's murder, Sheriff Winder spoke of the heinous crime. "Occasionally we encounter people who are evil," Winder said. "The individual who perpetrated this is nothing short of that."

Authorities in Utah hope to extradite Sansing to face murder charges. And they're looking at him in connection with other unsolved murders that occurred during 1989 to 1995, when he lived in Utah.

Fundamental Love

RULON JEFFS—"UNCLE RULON" TO THOUSANDS OF fundamentalist Mormons—lay dying. Some of his wives—believed to number 75—and some of his dozens of children were at his bedside. Among them was his 14th born child, Warren, who would become the third generation Jeffs to lead the Fundamentalist Church of Jesus Christ Latter-day Saints.

When his father finally took his last breath at age 93 in 2002, 45-year old Warren Jeffs succeeded him as the voice of God on Earth and leader of an estimated 10,000 members of the FLDS church, many of them girls and women trapped in a life of little education, marriage to much older men, and no way out.

Jeffs is the man Mormons—and non-Mormons—hate. He's the face of everything bad in fundamentalist Mormonism, famous for defying the LDS church by preaching polygamy, a practice the Mormons abandoned in the 1890s in exchange for Utah statehood.

He was born December 3, 1955 in Sacramento, Calif., but his story begins in Utah.

HE LOOKED MORE LIKE HOLLYWOOD'S IDEA OF A down-on-his-luck used car salesman than the man who had sex with dozens of girls and women—all in the name of God, of course.

Jeffs was thin and dark haired, with a long face and square jaw. He wore large glasses and a comb-over—until he went to prison and his hair was cut shorter.

He grew up outside of Salt Lake City. Before he became the voice of God on Earth, he served as the principal of Alta Academy, an FLDS private school in the area. It was not a very glamorous job with the FLDS, but he was known for being a stickler about rules and discipline. His father had changed the structure of the church, eliminating its council and placing himself as its only leader so Warren Jeffs not only became the group's new prophet, he gained control over its property holdings as well as its followers. Early on he married some of his father's wives, demanded women in the sect be completely subservient to men, "reassigned" wives to other men at whim, and banned laughing.

As if there was much to laugh about.

He married off young girls to men old enough to be their fathers or grandfathers, and dictated nearly every aspect of the members' lives, from the clothes they wore to whom they could marry to what toys children could play with. He insisted on no television and no Internet.

Among his advice to women:

> *Ladies, build up your husband by being submissive. That's how you will give your children success; you will want your children to be obedient, to be submissive to righteous living.*

He also made outrageous comments about race, including:

> *The black race is the people through which the devil has always been able to bring evil unto the earth.*

THE FLDS IS NOT THE ONLY FUNDAMENTALIST Mormon off-shoot, but it's one of the largest.

For a couple of brief years after Warren Jeffs took power, many of the FLDS lived in a compound he had established in West Texas he named Yearning for Zion, or the YFZ Ranch, 1,700 acres dominated by a huge white temple. The ranch was near Colorado City, AZ, on the border of Arizona and Utah. FLDS members also lived in sister cities Centennial Park, AZ and Hildale, Utah.

Once upon a time children attended public schools, but they closed after FLDS members opened their own schools. Many children on the compounds have minimal home-schooling—with no oversight by the state—and often can't read or write. Young boys work as slave labor in construction and families raise horses and livestock. The poverty level in the communities is high; the residents of the FLDS compounds in Arizona are the state's largest population receiving food stamps.

For girls there is only one goal: motherhood. Girls who have left FLDS say they looked forward to motherhood—but dreaded marriage to men they didn't know or love.

Interviewed several months after she fled the ranch with her mother and sisters, one teenager talked of having her hair cut for the first time, going to school, and making friends. If she was still at the ranch, she would be groomed to be a young bride—a very young one.

"It's all about the men," she told a reporter when she described the FLDS way of life. "We have to love them no matter what. They're pompous asses.

"The husband puts religion over family," she explained.

SOME CALL THEM "AMERICA'S LAST PIONEERS." America is fascinated with them.

There are the scripted television shows, including the HBO hit, "Big Love," about a fictional fundamentalist Mormon family—handsome dad, three pretty wives, and cute kids. The show's creators said they wanted to show "a fair portrayal of polygamy in America without being judgmental."

Reality shows like "Sister Wives" (a man, his four wives and 16 children - at last count), and "My Five Wives" (husband, five wives, 24 children), both on TLC, present families that, all in all, are pretty dull—except for curiosity about their sex lives.

Fundamentalists believe that God commands them to practice polygamy. The wives—at least the ones that let cameras in—say it's what they want.

Men want to know: just how do the sleeping arrangements work? Women want to know: what is so great about a guy that multiple women will share him? (And how do they decide who cooks and cleans up?)

There are fundamentalists....and then there are fundamentalists. Some—like the family on "Big Love"— are not members of a cult or religious community practicing polygamy. They have formed a kind of family that works for them. There are thousands of people in Utah and Arizona practicing polygamy who do not force girls into marriages.

The FLDS is not one of them. Warren Jeff's followers have no autonomy and are not given the freedom to choose their own spouses.

BY 2004, JUST TWO YEARS INTO HIS LEADERSHIP role, Warren Jeffs was in hot water. Male followers he had excommunicated (another whim) filed a civil suit against him that year, and a nephew took him to court, charging that his uncle had sexually assaulted him as a child.

The next year, Arizona authorities indicted Jeffs on charges of sexual conduct with a minor. In 2006 he faced two counts of rape as an accomplice for his role in arranging a marriage between a 14-year-old girl and her19-year-old cousin.

For years, Utah looked the other way, often not prosecuting polygamists or bigamists. Prosecutors were reluctant to file charges against consenting adults in a religious context. That began to change with the high-profile trial of Tom Green, who was convicted in 2001 of raping and impregnating one of his five wives when she was 13. Prosecutors alleged that Green practiced bigamy with underage girls, and at the same time scammed the state. He married teenagers, divorced them, and then collected the welfare payments they received as "single mothers" while he continued living with them. He was the first polygamist in fifty years to be prosecuted in Utah.

A few years later, as criminal charges started to mount against Jeffs, he dropped out of sight. Law enforcement assumed he was hiding out at various FLDS compounds and the FBI added him to its Ten Most Wanted list.

They caught him in Las Vegas in August, 2006 during a routine traffic stop. Jeffs was a passenger in a late-model SUV that was stopped by a state trooper for not displaying valid license plates. The trooper recognized Jeffs from wanted posters. He was carrying several cell phones, more than $50,000 in cash, and a stash of wigs and sunglasses in the car.

In 2007, Jeffs was tried and convicted in Utah on charges of being an accessory to rape. Two young women who escaped the ranch testified and helped to convict him.

When his 10-year sentence was overturned by the Utah Supreme Court in 2010, he was extradited to Texas where he faced charges for sexual assault of children stemming from a police raid at the ranch in 2008. During the raid authorities found a treasure trove of evidence against Jeffs and several other members of the FLDS in connection to their marriages to underage girls.

Jeffs went on trial in 2011 for two of his own "celestial marriages"—one with a 12-year-old girl and another with a 15-year-old girl who later had his child. Both of these so-called unions violated Texas law.

Like other sexual predators (see: Steven Powell, Jeffrey Epstein, Westley Allen Dodd, and many others), Jeff's diaries and tape recordings were part of his undoing.

Prosecutors in the sexual assault case presented a chilling recording of him having sex with the 12-year-old girl who he claims was his "spiritual wife."

The polygamist cult leader's voice can be clearly heard on the recording, ordering the little girl to "take your clothes off," as she is heard crying. Jeffs is then heard asking the child: "How do you feel, doesn't it feel good?"

The then-55-year-old continues to coach the girl throughout the ordeal, advising her to "just don't think about the pain." There appeared to be other people present in the room during the "marriage consummation" and prosecutors claim that women in the cult were holding the little girl down as Jeffs raped her.

At another juncture Jeffs is heard on the recording ordering the girl "to feel his presence...the spirit of God."

The bed he raped the girls on was made-to-order. Jeffs designed it to look like an altar, then had it placed on a tower of white limestone. It looked more like a casket without a lid than a marital bed.

During the trial jurors learned he had more than 70 illegal marriages, as many as a third of which were with underage girls.

This time he was convicted and sentenced to life in prison.

Warren Jeffs is locked away for the rest of his life. Yet, he finds ways to wield power from behind bars. After his first conviction, he "resigned" as president of the FLDS, but continued to consider himself the prophet, God's spokesman on Earth. He still banishes and ex-communicates members of FLDS for not following his edicts. He has ordered married couples not to have sex (the birth rate has dropped) and he testified on behalf of a woman in his cult that is fighting to keep custody of her children from their father who has left the FLDS.

He is housed in a prison in Palestine, Texas. It's only a few hours from the multi-million house he built for himself on the ranch, which now sits empty. It may as well be a million miles away.

Why don't more members leave? Why do members of FLDS blindly follow him, even as he sits in prison for heinous crimes?

Some say they still believe he is the prophet.

There have been several books written about Jeffs, and a Lifetime movie aired in June, 2014. One of the books, "Stolen Innocence," is by Elissa Wall who escaped from the sect and is suing Jeffs for $40 million.

She was the 14 year old Jeffs forced to marry her cousin. Wall testified against him at his Utah trial.

"Men were in charge of us," Wall wrote. "They were the only way we were going to get to Heaven. We had to love them no matter what... We had to share them with other women... We had to submit."

In 2008, hundreds of children were removed from the Yearning for Zion Ranch after the state received a phone call claiming a 16-year old girl at the ranch had been abused and that several underage girls were pregnant or married. The Texas State Supreme Court ruled the children were removed without a court order, and should be returned to the ranch. They never located the person who was the subject of the call.

AS EVIDENCE THAT TRUTH IS STRANGER THAN fiction, the mansion built by Jeffs' followers at his request in Hildale, Utah is now a bed-and-breakfast.

Willie Jessop, Jeffs' former bodyguard and a former spokesman for FLDS, bought the property for $3.6 million at an auction with money he won after he sued the church. He successfully charged that the church ruined his excavation business and harassed his family after he broke rank with FLDS and refused to defend Jeffs when he was arrested.

Jeffs never lived on the estate, which is surrounded by 12-foot high concrete walls. He was in prison by then.But his notoriety is part of the draw, hence the name "America's Most Wanted Suites and Bed & Breakfast." For the curious there are 14 rooms, and one king suite, featuring climate control, a smart TV and access to Wi-Fi. There's also a spa and an exercise room.

It's a good location, just a short drive from Zion National Park, Bryce Canyon National Park and the Grand Canyon.

Jessop said he took down seven "No Trespassing" signs around the property and replaced them with "Welcome Home" signs.

Utah's tourism board said it is cautiously optimistic about the project.

Killed While She Slept

IT'S BEEN TEN YEARS SINCE LORI HACKING WAS killed in her sleep. On the anniversary of one of the most high-profile murders in Utah, Lori Hacking's mother gave a rare interview to the Deseret News. Thelma Soares said she had forgiven her son-in-law, Mark Hacking, but will always feel the loss that began one morning in the summer of 2004.

"People say, 'You need to do this, you need to do that. You need to get over it.' I wanted to slap them," she said. "Because you never get over it....You get over the shock and the disbelief and all of that panic — that desperation you feel when you can't find your child. You get over that as time passes. But you never get over the loss."

Her daughter seemed poised to get everything she had ever wanted in life. Lori and Mark Hacking had been married five years. Lori loved her husband and she was excited when she told her family she was five weeks pregnant. She and Mark were packing up and preparing to move to Chapel Hill, N.C., where he would begin medical school.

The couple had a plan. Then, suddenly, Mark's plan included murdering Lori.

THELMA AND HERALD SOARES MET WHEN BOTH were serving as missionaries for the Church of Jesus Christ of Latter-day Saints. Herald was a native of Brazil, and after their mission they settled in Fullerton, Calif. where Herald taught high school Spanish and Portuguese. They adopted a girl and named her Lori Kay.

A few years later, they divorced and Thelma and Lori moved to Orem, Utah, about 40 miles south of Salt Lake City. Lori and Mark Hacking attended the same high school, but didn't meet until an outing at Lake Powell, a popular recreation area on the Colorado River on the border between Utah and Arizona.

According to family and friends, the two young people were inseparable. It was a real-life example of opposites attracting. Mark was outgoing, while Lori was more private and practical. It worked for them.

Lori could have had her pick of young men. With her long hair and ringlets, she resembled the actress Keri Russell. Mark was tall and muscular. His hair was thinning so he eventually shaved his head and sported a goatee.

"He adored her. And she adored him," Thelma Soares told "48 Hours." "I couldn't have asked for a better son-in-law. Lori used to call him 'My big, old teddy bear.'"

They married in 1999. Lori worked as a sales assistant in the brokerage department at Wells Fargo and Mark finished his education, graduating with honors and a degree in Psychology from the University of Utah. While he studied and prepared to apply to medical schools, he worked as a psychiatric aide, a job that permitted him to study during slow hours. Lori thought they should put off having children until Mark realized his dream of being accepted to medical school. He was contemplating a specialty in oncology.

Mark was the fifth of seven children. He was under stress to live up to the success the rest of his family had achieved. His father was a pediatrician and an uncle had been a plastic surgeon. Mark's two brothers were "high achievers," according to their father, Douglas Hacking, who said Mark felt pressure to excel, too.

Mark was well liked by his parent's friends. He taught Sunday school. He was attentive to Lori and often sent her flowers.

Outwardly, Mark seemed to be succeeding. But he always seemed to lack the self-discipline needed to reach his dreams. There was a kind of façade to him, a face he put on for others. His mother said he was outgoing with people, but didn't seem to be comfortable with himself and his feelings.

In retrospect, there were warning signs about his behavior. He smoked cigarettes and drank alcohol—both prohibited in the Mormon Church—and reportedly had sex while he was on his mission in Canada. He was sent home early for disciplinary reasons. (Mormon men and women are expected to wait until marriage to have sex.) His mother says that when Mark came home from Canada, he seemed to be depressed and he went to see a counselor about it. "He told the counselor he was feeling down on himself because of mistakes," she says. She thinks he ended therapy too soon.

At the time his mission was cut short he had been dating Lori for about three years. One of her closest friends said Lori was upset about the incident and she stopped seeing Mark for a while.

But soon they grew close again.

Later his family—and his defense attorney—would theorize that his alleged mental illness began when he fell from a roof in his early 20s, sustaining a head injury.

Who knows why someone builds lie upon lie, until they're too many of them and they topple.

Mark had his college degree. He spent their savings visiting medical schools he might want to apply to. He said he was accepted at four medical schools. He chose the University of North Carolina in Chapel Hill and the couple traveled to the town to rent a place to live.

Back home, Lori, now 27, quit her job and began to pack up their apartment. Just like they had hoped and planned, Lori learned she was pregnant. At a family party in June, Mark, 28, showed off a new stethoscope he planned to take with him to medical school in the fall.

Three days before she disappeared, Lori received a phone call at work that left her in tears. Had she learned that her husband was a pathological liar?

THEY MUST HAVE ARGUED THE NIGHT OF JULY 18, 2004.

Lori learned from the fateful phone call that they wouldn't be moving to North Carolina—that her husband had fabricated his college education, his studying for entrance to medical school, his acceptance at two schools, his admission to one, his plans to become an oncologist. Everything was a lie.

On the morning of July 19, Mark Hacking called Lori's office at Wells Fargo and was told that she hadn't shown up for work. Then he called police to say that his wife had gone jogging and hadn't come home. He said he had been searching for her. No one knew it then, but he had really been shopping for a new mattress.

Police told him it was too early for them to consider her missing, and suggested he check with local hospitals and friends.

Family members, friends and Lori's colleagues helped search Memory Grove and City Creek Canyon, the area northeast of downtown Salt Lake City where Lori liked to jog.

Lori's family—and Mark—held a press conference and distributed posters with her photo. Mark told the media that Lori often went jogging early in the morning and let him sleep. He said he often drove her to work, but on that morning she had driven herself. He had tried to call her about 10 a.m. to say hello, and learned she hadn't shown up for work.

The community got involved, taking on the search for Lori. Except for her car, found near the trail head, there no sign of her. Lori and Mark's families held out hope. It was two years since Elizabeth Smart had been abducted from her home. She had been found after nine months. Maybe Lori would be found, too.

By now it was a police matter, and when they discovered that Mark had spun one breathtaking lie after another suspicion fell on him.

Although for three years he had supposedly studied, packed his backpack with books and set off to classes, and even had his mother-in-law help him with term papers, he was not attending classes. In fact, he never graduated from the University of Utah and was never admitted to medical school in North Carolina. The phone call that left Lori in tears, believed to be a call back from the medical school, may have been her first indication that Mark was not the man she thought he was.

If he could lie about college, what else could he be lying about? He assured both families that he had nothing to do with Lori's disappearance.

One day after Lori was reported missing, police were called to a disturbance at the Chase Suite Hotel about a half-mile from the Hackings' apartment. Police found Mark Hacking running around naked except for a pair of shoes. His family checked him in to the psychiatric unit at University Hospital.

To this day no one knows if he had a true psychotic break—or was faking a breakdown just as he had faked the previous several years.

On July 24, confronted by his father and his brothers, Mark admitted that he had killed Lori and dumped her body in a trash bin. They took the information to the police and for the next several weeks the search was focused at the Salt Lake County landfill. Mark arrested on suspicion of aggravated murder, soon to become first degree murder charges.

Police pieced together Lori's last hours.

Sometime Sunday night or Monday morning, Mark shot Lori while she was asleep with a .22 caliber rifle. He wrapped her body in trash bags, and drove her body to a Dumpster. A surveillance tape showed Mark entering a store to buy cigarettes, checking his hands and fingers, and then driving away in his wife's car just minutes after the time they believe Lori died.

Then he left her car near the trail where she liked to jog. Lori's blood was in the car and the driver's seat had been adjusted to fit a tall person—she was 5'4"—Mark was 6'. Her car keys weren't in the car—they were found in the apartment.

Police also found a receipt for a new queen-sized mattress and went looking for one that had been disposed of. They found it cut up and in a trash bin near the University of Utah hospital where Mark worked.

They also found a bloody knife in the apartment and blood on the headboard of the couple's bed, but they never found the rifle used to shoot Lori.

They did find a note Lori had left behind, probably written just a day or two before her death:

> *"I hate coming home from work because it hurts to be home in our apartment...I can't imagine life with you if things don't change. I got someone I don't want to spend the rest of my life with unless changes are made."*

ON AUGUST 14, 2004 A MEMORIAL SERVICE FOR LORI took place at the LDS Windsor Stake Center in Orem, Utah. More than 600 people attended the service. Her wedding dress was displayed, as was a poster-sized photograph of her. Donations were received to help with the ongoing search effort.

The two families grieved together. Mark's father gave the opening prayer. *The Salt Lake Tribune* reported that he said, "We truly appreciate the influence [Lori] has had in our lives...We've all been touched by her in some way...We hope she can feel our love for her today."Both families struggled with why Mark deceived them all with his lies. One brother, a computer engineer, speculated there was a mundane explanation. Maybe Mark missed the deadline for registering for school and once he told people he was going, the lies escalated.

Lori Hacking's badly decomposed body was found in early October under tons of compact garbage. An autopsy could not confirm if she was pregnant.

At first, Mark plead not guilty. In April, 2005 he changed his plea to guilty in exchange for a lesser sentence.

At his sentencing, Mark wept as he spoke:

"I killed her and my unborn child. I put them in the garbage. I can't explain why I did it. I know I wasn't myself that night, but that's no excuse. I am tormented every waking minute for what I have done. I deserve to be in prison, probably for the rest of my life."

Thelma Soares, Lori's mother, also cried as she read a statement in court about the loss of her beloved daughter and her unborn grandchild.

"He now tells me he's sorry, but his words ring hollow," she told the judge. Then she addressed Mark Hacking directly.

"How could you do that, Mark? How could you do that to me?"

Mark replied, "I'm sorry."

On June 6, 2005, Mark Hacking was sentenced to six years to life in prison. People were outraged at the sentence, but it was the maximum the judge could give under Utah law. Although he called him "the poster boy for dishonesty," the judge's hands were tied. Under Utah's system of indeterminate criminal sentences, first-degree felony murder brings a mandatory five years to life, but Hacking's minimum is increased to six years because he used a firearm. The distress this caused—that Mark Hacking *could* be eligible for parole after just six years—led to change. In 2006, Utah legislators passed House Bill 102, also known as "Lori's Law." It increases the minimum penalty for a person convicted for first degree murder to fifteen years to life.

Mark Hacking will have his first date with the parole board in August, 2034.

Two scholarships in Lori's memory help young women at the colleges she attended, Weber State University in Ogden, and at the University of Utah in Salt

Lake City. The only criteria is that they have escaped from domestic violence or have overcome other difficult circumstances.

Thelma Soares had the Hacking name removed from her daughter's gravestone. It now has the name she was born with, "Lori Kay Soares," and then the word "Filhinha"—Portuguese for "little daughter."

Soares said she doesn't feel the anger she once did. She even corresponds occasionally with the man who killed her daughter. She shared one of Mark Hacking's letters to her with the Deseret News:

"I hope your health as well as your peace and happiness continue to improve. I think of you often, but I never know what to write... I remember your kindness and acceptance from the time I first met you... I remember the love you showed even when I didn't deserve it. I remember your fear when I told everyone Lori was missing, the anger and despair in your letters and on the day I was sentenced. I am sorry. I know I have said/written that many times, always sincerely. But with less understanding. Sorry is another inadequate term, but I feel that sorrow to my bones."

In addition to exchanging letters with Hacking, Soares also frequently exchanges emails with members of his family.

"They're a wonderful family. They don't come any better than that family and the kids," she said. "He was just this good kid," she said. "The problem with Mark was he suffered from depression."

While forgiving her son-in-law "doesn't make anything that he did right," Soares said she did it for her own sake, not for his.

"People have so many different ideas of what forgiveness means. And I guess it means different things to different people. Does it mean what I think he did was OK? Of course not!

"I'm the one who's benefited from that, not him. I mean, he's still in prison. He said in other letters — he calls them monstrous, hideous things that he did — 'I should never get out of here. I don't deserve to get out of here.' He thinks he should be in there for his life."

So does everyone else who knew and loved Lori.

Afterword

MARK HACKING'S FAMILY RELEASED A STATEMENT on June 6, 2005, the day he was sentenced. It was read by his father, Douglas Hacking, at a press conference in Salt Lake City:

"It is difficult to talk about our son, Mark Hacking, without sounding like we are making excuses for his involvement in the senseless and tragic death of our daughter-in-law Lori on the night of July 18, 2004. We are doing so to clear up some misconceptions about this case and to provide a clearer understanding of what occurred and why.

"As has already been reported by the media, in 1996 Mark was sent home from an LDS mission for failing to live up to the high standards expected from the missionaries called to represent the church. He was also having some health problems and returned ashamed and in spiritual, emotional, and physical pain.

"Within a few weeks, Mark suffered a series of additional health problems that resulted in three surgeries. The most serious of these issues was a concussion, seizure and broken back from falling off the roof of a house. Following months of incapacitating back pain, Mark tried to go back to college but found it almost impossible to sit in class for long due to the pain and resulting inability to concentrate. His ability to sit improved over the years, but his inability to concentrate or learn continued to hinder him.

"Although we were unaware of Mark's learning disability, we have recently come to know how agonizing it was for him to fail one class after another to the point that he could no longer attend college. These failures were terribly hard on his self-esteem and created constant anxiety for him. Rather than admit to himself and others that he could not succeed in college, he began to create the illusion that he was going to school and doing well. He pretended to graduate from the University of Utah and carried his deception to the point of actually visiting several medical schools to 'interview.' We now know that he lied about graduating from college and applying to medical schools. Mark told everyone that he had been accepted to four schools and deliberated which to attend. Last summer, Mark and Lori traveled to North Carolina to look for a place to live and signed a rental agreement. They then quit their jobs in Utah and packed to move.

"Mark sensed that the house of cards he had been building for years was beginning to sway, and he became even more anxious. Lori found out that he had never applied to any medical schools, and Mark finally admitted everything to her on the night of July 18, 2004. As you can imagine, Lori was deeply hurt.

"To clear up some misconceptions about Mark's confession, it was reported Mark's brothers, Lance and Scott, were the ones who told authorities Mark had killed Lori. The reality is that on July 24, Lance confronted Mark with the evidence police had gathered and urged him to reveal where Lori's body was. He and Scott met with Mark that evening, at which time Mark confessed everything to them. His attorney was notified and instructed, by Mark, to provide information regarding Lori's whereabouts to the district attorney, an act which took place the following day. From that point on, it was never a matter of whether Mark would plead guilty but when he would do it based on the processes of the legal system. Mark resolved in August that he would never let his case be tried and informed his attorney of that decision.

"As for Mark's character, until this chain of events, he had never been in trouble with the law nor did he ever develop bad habits such as the use of illegal drugs. Mark always had good friends. He has always been an obedient, hardworking, and thoughtful individual who treated us with respect.

"More than anything, we know that Mark loved Lori. We never heard them argue. We never heard him say a negative word about her. When they were not working, they were inseparable.

"Mark suffers continually for his choices. Anyone who could have shared in our conversations with him or read his letters and life history would know the depth of his sorrow and remorse for having taken the life of the one person he cherished most and for having caused pain to so many others especially Lori's family. Mark was close to Thelma and has expressed particular concern for her suffering in almost every letter and conversation we have had with him.

"We are not sure any of us will ever understand why Mark did what he did, nor are we sure he will ever fully understand it either. What we are sure about is that he is willing to pay any price for what he has done. He has a desire to continue to serve others but realizes his opportunities to do so in prison will be limited. As a family, we hope that someday he can be released from prison so that he can be in a better position to contribute to the lives of others. As for when Mark should be released, we will leave that up to the parole board as they consider how he conducts his life while incarcerated. And for the eternal consequences of his actions we will leave that to the savior, who will judge him with perfect justice but also perfect mercy, having a full knowledge of the state of his mind at the time he ended Lori's life.

"Our family continues to feel deep sorrow and regret for Thelma, Herald, Paul, and Lori's other family members and friends for the emptiness that has filled their lives since losing Lori. As parents, we wish we could have prevented this tragic event. We also loved her and will continue to miss her presence in our lives as well.

"Although we abhor what Mark did, we are proud of him for taking responsibility for his actions and for his desire to repent. As hard as it may seem to believe, we love him more now than before.

"We wish to express a final thanks to our own family, friends, neighbors, and community members that have extended unconditional, Christ-like love to our family during this devastating time. Thank you also to Mr. Gil Athay for his help and professionalism in providing services to Mark.

"We are grateful that the media has respected our wishes for privacy over the past year. This will be our final statement to the press, as we request that we be permitted to move on with our lives.

"Finally, in the hope that someone else might learn from Mark's mistakes, permit us to quote Mark:

"'I know prison is where I need to be. I will spend my time there doing all I can to right the many wrongs I have done, though I realize complete atonement is impossible in this life. I have a lot of healing and changing to do, but I hope that someday I can become the man Lori always thought I was.

"'To the many people I have hurt, I am more sorry than you could ever know. Every day my soul burns in

torment when I think of what you must be going through. I wish I could take away your pain. I wish I could take back all the lies I have told and replace them with the truth. I wish I could put Lori back into your arms. My pain is deserved; yours is not. From the bottom of my heart, I beg for your forgiveness.

"'There is no such thing as a harmless lie no matter how small it is. You may think a lie only hurts the liar, but this is far from the truth. If you are traveling a path of lies, please stop now and face the consequences. Whatever those consequences, they will be better than the pain you are causing yourself and others.'"

"If I Die, It May Not Be an Accident"

THE WORDS WERE SCRAWLED ON A SINGLE PIECE OF lined notebook paper. In her sweet, girlish handwriting, Susan Powell wrote of her fears and hopes for her children, then locked the note in her safe-deposit box at a bank.

On the outside, she wrote:

> *For family, friends of Susan all except for Josh Powell husband, I don't trust him!*

Inside, she wrote:

> *I want it documented somewhere that there is extreme turmoil in our marriage.*

For mine [sic] and my children's safety I feel the need to have a paper trail… which would not be accessible to my husband… it is an open fact that we have life insurance policies of over a million if we die in the next four years.

If I die, it may not be an accident even if it looks like one.

> *Take care of my boys.*

It was signed and dated June 28, 2008. Susan Powell was leaving a clue, in case of her premature death.

But when it was found in late 2009, something just as terrible had happened.

She had vanished.

Over the next two and a half years, as America's largest missing persons investigation proved fruitless, her husband Josh would flee their Utah home for the bunker-like atmosphere of his father Steve's house in their hometown of Puyallup, Washington. Walls, fences and surveillance cameras protected Josh. He never helped search for her, and neither did the man who had been sexually obsessed with her for years, her father-in-law, Steve. Her young sons, starved for love and attention, began to act out. Her parents and sisters would know unbelievable heartache. And the only people who knew the secret to her disappearance would kill themselves.

If today was a Sunday, and Josh Powell was scheduled for a home visitation with his sons, they would arrive and run into the house, just as they did on February 5, 2012.

Troubled because an on-going custody fight over Charlie and Braden, just four and three years old respectively when their mother disappeared, and by police in two states watching him, Josh took the coward's way out. After being ordered to undergo a psychosexual evaluation and a polygraph, Josh killed himself and his sons in a deliberately set house explosion and fire.

The West Valley City, Utah Police Department continued its investigation into Susan's disappearance for another year, then closed the case in May, 2013 finally releasing thousands of pages of documents her family had been denied access to.

After the boys' deaths and the closing of the police investigation, both Utah and Washington State reviewed the policies that permitted a person of interest in a murder case to have visitation with his sons.

A Washington state panel reviewing the deaths of the Powell boys concluded that the police and the Department of Social and Health Services—Child Protective Services—failed to communicate with each other about the danger Josh posed to Charlie and Braden.

DSHS HADN'T TOLD THE PIERCE COUNTY (Washington) Sheriff's Department that Josh was allowed to see his children at his rental house, a much less secure environment than the office of the Foster Care Resource Network, which provided a caseworker. And because Utah sealed its records and WVCPD kept its case file on Susan's disappearance closed, Washington didn't know about the letter Susan had locked in her safe deposit box, or that Susan's blood had been found in her W. Sarah Circle home. It wasn't until late 2011 that authorities in Washington learned that pornographic images with incest themes had been found on Josh's computer—evidence that likely would have kept Josh from having home visitations with his sons. It wasn't until 2014 that documents showed the FBI knew of the pornography, too.

A spokeswoman for DSHS said the agency would have gone back to court to negotiate visitations if they had any indication that Josh was suicidal.

They *did* know.

The proof is in the thick divorce documents of Josh's parents from the early 1990s, in which his teenage suicide attempt is mentioned. It was part of the DSHS file. The psychiatrist assigned to evaluate Josh, Dr. James Manley, addressed it in his lengthy report on Josh.

They all knew.

The state review panel recommended that staff re-think visitation agreements when a psychosexual evaluation is ordered. With the backing of Chuck and Judy Cox, Susan's parents, the Washington legislature considered, but has not yet adopted, a bill that would restrict or block visitation rights for someone who is the subject of a murder investigation.

The Coxes filed a $20 million dollar claim against DSHS, accusing the agency of negligence in the deaths of Charlie and Braden. The suit says that DSHS knew, or should have known, about the danger posed to the children. Another suit is aimed at preventing Josh's sister, Alina, and mother from benefiting from his and Susan's life insurance.

Other agencies involved in the Powell case have come under self-scrutiny, but again, not much has changed. The 911 dispatcher who mishandled the call from the foster care caseworker on February 5, 2012 received a written reprimand. It took eight minutes for him to send a police car, and thirteen minutes for the car to arrive at the house. His supervisor wrote that the 18-year veteran had "violated several department policies" and failed to recognize "red flags" that could have led to a faster response. Odds are it still would not have made a difference and saved the lives of Charlie and Braden. (The transcript of the 911 call appears at the end of this chapter.)

FCRN, where the caseworker was employed, has studied its policies to see if the deaths of Charlie and Braden could have been prevented. "I must have asked a thousand people 'what could we have done differently?'" FCRN's executive director Lyn Okarski said. "No one could tell us. We are a little more cautious about home visits."

THE QUESTION THAT LINGERS FOR SUSAN'S PARENTS is why wasn't Josh arrested, and could his sons have been saved?

After expressing his shock and sorrow at the events of February 5, 2012 and calling Josh's actions "evil," West Valley City Police Chief Buzz Nielsen said they hadn't arrested Josh because they were still building their case when he killed the boys and himself. Nielsen said that because Susan's body had never been found, they had to build a stronger case against Josh.

But prosecutors in Washington state say that, based on the same evidence, *they* would have charged Josh for Susan's murder.

Putting together a criminal case without a body is difficult, but far from impossible. It has even been done successfully more than once in Utah. It requires a mountain of circumstantial evidence, which Washington State authorities insisted Utah had from day one.

Within a week or two after Susan disappeared, the West Valley City police knew it was her blood found near the love seat in the house. They found Susan's cellphone in Josh's minivan. They knew Josh had changed his story about where he'd been, first telling his sister he was at work, and then explaining how he and the boys went camping. They knew that two days after Susan went missing, Josh mysteriously rented a car and drove for 800 miles. And police found Susan's letter in a safe deposit box stating that if anything happened to her, even if it looked like an accident, it was not. They knew about the cartoon porn found on

Josh's computer, a predilection which could endanger the children. They knew Josh had emptied Susan's IRA account. And they knew the boys were beginning to remember and talk about their mother going camping but not coming home with them.

Josh had made the pancakes that may have sickened Susan Sunday afternoon. He had a tarp, shovel and gas can in the back of his minivan. He had taken out a lot of life insurance on Susan.

Police knew—because Charlie had told them—that Susan's whereabouts was a "big secret."

Susan's best friend, Kiirsi Hellewell, thinks WVCPD's biggest mistake occurred on the first night, December 7, 2009, when they let Josh return to the house with his sons after a brief conversation at the police department. There's no law that the children of a man whose wife is missing should be taken from him—even after he becomes a person of interest. But maybe there should be. Maybe, as Kiirsi suggests, if your spouse is missing, you don't get your kids back until you've cooperated in every way and been ruled out as a suspect.

Beginning in 2010 Susan's parents considered their legal options. At one point lawyer Anne Bremner indicated a wrongful death suit against Josh was an option—much like the family of Ronald Goldman brought against O.J. Simpson—but the family preferred the police do what they needed to do to charge Josh with a crime. They wanted to be on the side of the police, who were telling them regularly that an arrest was imminent. The Coxes feared the police would stop looking for Susan if they didn't do everything asked of them.

But nothing happened. And with that inaction, comes second-guessing. If Josh had been arrested on any charge—kidnapping, jaywalking, or a parking ticket—would Charlie and Braden still be alive?

WHEN LORI HACKING WENT MISSING—REPORTEDLY during a morning jog on July 19, 2004 in an area northeast of downtown Salt Lake City—Josh and Susan were spending their first summer in West Valley City, Utah. They had purchased a home in a neighborhood of other young, Mormon families.

It was hot and Susan, who was studying for her financial broker's license, spent a lot of time at Kiirsi's home down the street. They probably discussed the missing woman, said to be five weeks pregnant. Susan was three months pregnant.

Susan was new to Utah, but long-time residents had experience helping look for missing people. Thousands turned out to help search for Elizabeth Smart when the 14-year old was kidnapped from her bedroom in her house in Salt Lake City in June 2002 and rejoiced when she was found nine months later. In the summer of 2004, they were helping again. Hundreds were walking the Memory Grove and City Creek Canyon areas where Lori Hacking was said to have gone for a jog and never returned home. Within days, police focused on a trail of lies Mark Hacking had told his wife, his family, and to them. He eventually pleaded guilty to shooting his wife with a rifle and leaving her body in a Dumpster. Her remains were found in a landfill after weeks of digging.

There weren't the organized searches for Susan that there had been for Elizabeth Smart and Lori Hacking. The West Valley City Police wanted to handle it themselves. And where would people look? There was no park or neighborhood or jogging trail where she was last seen.

Instead, there were thousands of abandoned mine shafts and hundreds of miles of desert in all directions.

After Susan disappeared, the husband of a co-worker remembered a Christmas party in 2008 when Josh talked about his fascination with TV crime investigation shows. He discussed "how to kill someone, dispose of the body, and not get caught," and told the partygoer that Utah's thousands of mine shafts and tunnels was the perfect place to "dispose of someone and no one would ever search for the body."

He bragged to a friend—before Susan went missing—with the same bravado he talked about TV shows that Mark Hacking had made mistakes. Those might have included leaving her body in a place it could be found, speaking to the media, and sticking around. Better to hide a body where it would *never* be found, keep your mouth shut, and move away.

In his own psychopathic way, Josh was smarter than Mark Hacking. He left no crime scene. In fact, there was no proof that Susan had been murdered. Josh didn't have to try to dispose of a bloody mattress.

Like Mark Hacking, Josh lied about finishing college. Like Mark Hacking, Josh called Susan's cell phone on a ruse, knowing all along she couldn't answer because she was dead. Like Mark Hacking, Josh was feeling trapped by expectations he couldn't live up to. Like Lori, Susan had worked at Wells Fargo. Like Lori, Susan believed she was pregnant just before she vanished. Like Lori, Susan wrote a letter to her husband imploring him to make changes.

Like Mark Hacking, Josh was guilty of domestic violence.

LITTLE HAS BEEN SAID ABOUT THE ROLE OF domestic violence in what happened to Susan Powell.

Josh, after all, didn't strike Susan. Not that anyone knew of, anyway. Susan did tell a sister that she and Josh had once shoved each other. The police had never been called out to their home in West Valley City. Susan hadn't been treated at an emergency room. But, as most know, domestic violence isn't just physical. It's emotional, sexual and psychological and is more about control and power than hitting. Josh excelled at control and power.

Rather than the traditional profile of a man who abuses his wife, Josh fit a pattern of men who commit familicide—men who murder their entire families. The men are over-controlling, and—as Dr. Manley's evaluation of Josh pointed out—highly narcissistic. They sense that their power or control is ebbing and they feel diminished. The beginning of the end is when the woman tries to leave. Josh had certainly killed Susan. When it looked like he would never have custody of his sons again—when he had no power or control left—he killed them, too.

Could Susan's church, The Church of Jesus Christ of Latter-day Saints, or the Coxes or Susan's friends, have done more to intervene in her marriage? The Coxes felt it was Susan's decision alone whether to leave Josh or stay. Susan's bishop in Utah knew about her fears and unhappiness because she had talked to him about Josh. He assured her that she had tried everything she could to make her marriage happier. All of Susan's friends knew and encouraged her to leave him. Josh and Susan had some counseling through the LDS church, but Josh was not cooperating. He knew for at least two years that Susan was thinking of divorce. What Susan didn't know during that same time was that he was fantasizing that she was dead.

A few months after Josh killed his sons and himself, Chief Nielsen cryptically said his department was looking at "others" to charge in connection with Susan's disappearance. We now know that the "others" meant Josh's younger brother, Michael Powell. He killed himself in February, 2013, after learning that the police were focusing on a car he had abandoned in Oregon about two weeks after Susan disappeared. He had apparently helped Josh move Susan's body.

With Michael dead, that leaves Steve Powell, who must know what happened to Susan. But Steve, whose arrest on voyeurism charges touched off the custody battle for Charlie and Braden, is out of prison, and just another registered sex offender. The State of Washington has reinstated pornography charges against him that were dismissed when he was tried for voyeurism—that *could* be a reason for him to cooperate with investigators and say what he knows about Susan's disappearance, but it wasn't the last time he faced prison.

Susan has never been found. Chuck Cox is conducting his own search now. He wonders if there is anyone left to bring to justice.

Only time will tell.

To read the definitive account of Susan Powell's disappearance, see *If I Can't Have You—Susan Powell, Her Mysterious Disappearance and the Murder of Her Children*, by Gregg Olsen and Rebecca Morris. Published by St. Martin's Press. Available in hardcover, ebook and audio book. Paperback coming 2015.

Afterword

THE TRANSCRIPT OF THE CONVERSATION BETWEEN Charlie and Braden's caseworker and a 911 dispatcher on February 5, 2012 is heartbreaking to hear and to read. The dispatcher had nearly 20 years on the job, but that morning he couldn't see the forest for the trees. His department said he failed to recognize "red flags" that could have led have led to a faster response. Precious minutes passed as the dispatcher seems stuck in minutiae, like the color of the caseworker's car and a physical description of Josh. Later, the dispatcher said of course he knew who Josh Powell was; Josh was often in the news. But the dispatcher didn't seem to hear the caseworker explain who Josh was, and that he had just lost an important court decision. Experts say odds are a faster response might not have saved the lives of Charlie and Braden.

911 Operator: Good morning.

Caseworker: Hey, I'm on a supervised visitation for a court-ordered visit and something really weird is happened. The kids went into the house and the parent, the biological parent, his name is Josh Powell, will not let me in the door. What should I do?

911 Operator: What's the address?

Caseworker: It's 8119 and I think its 89th -- I don't know what the address is.

911 Operator: OK, that's pretty important for me to know.

Caseworker: I'm sorry, just a minute. Let me get in my car and see if I can find it. Nothing like this has ever happened before in these visitations, so, I'm really shocked and I can hear one of the kids crying but he still wouldn't let me in. OK, it is one, uh, one ... Oh, just a minute I have it here. You can't find me by GPS?

911 Operator: No.

Caseworker: OK, it is - I still can't find it. But I think I need help right away. He's on a very short leash with DSHS (Department of Social and Health Services), and CPS (Child Protective Services) has been involved. And this is the craziest thing. He looked right at me and closed the door. Are you there?

911 Operator: Yes, ma'am, I'm just waiting to know where you are.

Caseworker: OK. It's 8119 189th St. Court East, Puyallup, 98375. And I'd like to pull out of the driveway because I smell gasoline and he won't let me in.

911 Operator: You want to pull out of the driveway because you smell gasoline but he won't let you ...?

Caseworker: He won't let me in.

911 Operator: He won't let you out of the driveway?

Caseworker: He won't let me in the house.

911 Operator: Whose house is it?

Caseworker: He's got the kids in the house and he won't let me in. It's a supervised visit.

911 Operator: I understand. Whose house is it?

Caseworker: Josh Powell.

911 Operator: OK. You don't live there, right?

Caseworker: No. No. I'm contracted to the state to provide supervised visitation.

911 Operator: I see. OK. And who is there to exercise the visitation?

Caseworker: I am, uh, and the visit is with Josh Powell. And he's the husband of ...

911 Operator: And who's supervising?

Caseworker: I supervise.

911 Operator: So you supervise and you're doing the visit? You supervise yourself?

Caseworker: I supervise myself. I'm the supervisor here.

911 Operator: Wait a minute. If it's a supervised visit you can't supervise yourself if you're the visitor.

Caseworker: I supervise myself. I'm the supervisor for a supervised visit.

911 Operator: OK, but aren't you the one making the visit? Or is there another parent there that you're supervising?

Caseworker: I'm the one that supervises. I pick up the kids at their grandparents'.

911 Operator: Yes. And then who visits with the children?

Caseworker: Josh Powell.

911 Operator: OK. So, you're supposed to be there to supervise Josh Powell's visit with the children?

Caseworker: Yes, that's correct. And he's the husband of missing Susan Powell. This is a high-profile case.

911 Operator: How did he gain access to the children before you got there?

Caseworker: I was one step in back of them.

911 Operator: So they went into the house and he locked you out?

Caseworker: Yes. He shut the door right in my face.

911 Operator: Alright, now it's clear. Your last name?....

(Exchange in which caller provides personal information.)

911 Operator: And what agency are you with?

Caseworker: Foster Care Resource Network. (Pause). And the kids have been in there by now approximately 10 minutes. And he knows this is a supervised visit.

911 Operator: How many children?

Caseworker: Two, Braden is five and Charlie is seven.

911 Operator: And the dad's last name?

(Long Pause)

Caseworker: Powell. P-O-W-E-L-L.

911 Operator: Two L's? Two L's at the end of Powell?

Caseworker: Yes.

911 Operator: His first name?

Caseworker: His first name is Josh.

911 Operator: Black, white, Asian, Hispanic, Native?

Caseworker: He's white.

911 Operator: Date of birth?

Caseworker: I don't know. He's about 39. (He was 34.)

911 Operator: How tall?

Caseworker: 5' 10", 150 pounds.

911 Operator: Hair color?

Caseworker: Brown.

911 Operator: Did you notice what he was wearing?

Caseworker: No, I didn't notice what he was wearing.

911 Operator: Is he alone?

Caseworker: I don't know. I couldn't get into the house.

911 Operator: Are you in a vehicle now or on foot?

Caseworker: I'm in a vehicle. I'm in a Prius. A 2010 Prius. The door is locked. He hasn't opened the door. I rang the doorbell and everything. I begged him to let me in.

911 Operator: Please listen to my questions. What color is the Toyota Prius?

Caseworker: Gray. Dark gray.

911 Operator: And the license number?

Caseworker: I don't know I can look...
(she gets out of the car and then tells him the license number)

911 Operator: Alright, we'll have somebody look for you there.

Caseworker: OK. How long will it be?

911 Operator: I don't know, ma'am. They have to respond to emergency, life-threatening situations first. The first available deputy will respond.

Caseworker: This could be life-threatening. He went to court on Wednesday, and he didn't bring his kids back and this is really...I'm afraid for their lives.

911 Operator: OK. Has he threatened the lives of the children previously?

Caseworker: I have no idea.

911 Operator: Alright. Well, we'll have the first available deputy contact you.

Caseworker: Thank you.

A moment later, the caseworker smelled gasoline, got into her car, and backed it out of the driveway and away from the house. She heard some pops from the house, a loud whoosh, and then a boom. She felt her Prius rock on its wheels. At 12:16 p.m. the house exploded.

The caseworker called 911 a second time. This time a different dispatcher answered. The caseworker explained that a house with a man and two children inside was on fire. She was put on hold while the operator called the fire department. And then she had to explain again what the circumstances were. Finally, she heard the sirens of fire engines. By then, she was in tears.

PHOTO ARCHIVE

Baby Killer Photos

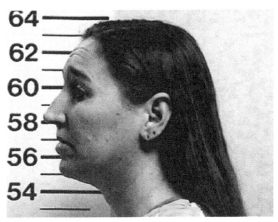

Megan Huntsman, after her arrest for allegedly killing her newborn infants and hiding them.

Megan Huntsman's husband, Darren West, said he had not known she had been pregnant, given birth seven times, and hid each infant in a box in the garage.

Deadly Distraction Photos

Prosecutors decided not to charge April Suwyn for the death of her daughter, Skyah.

Police say Justin Ross Harris wanted a "child free life" so he deliberately left his son, Cooper, to die in the car.

Leanna Harris called her husband "a wonderful father."

The Lego Murder Photos

Lucille Johnson's murder was finally solved by a fingerprint on a Lego.

Trudy Calabrese was volunteering, delivering boxes of food to families in need, when she was brutally murdered.

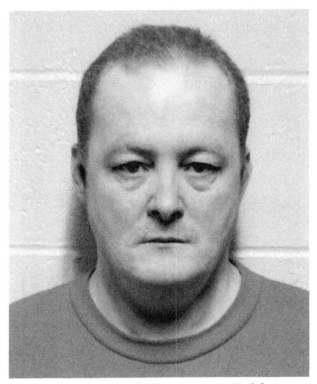

John Sansing is on death row in Arizona. Utah hopes to extradite him and prosecute him for the murder of Lucille Johnson.

Kara Sansing chatted with Trudy Calabrese when she arrived with donations of food for the family, then looked on as her husband committed rape and murder.

Fingerprints on Legos left at Lucille Johnson's house helped solve her murder.

Fundamental Love Photos

Warren Jeffs became leader of 10,000 members of the FLDS church when he succeed his father as the voice of God on Earth.

Jeffs built a temple at the 1,700 acre compound in West Texas named Yearning for Zion, or the YFZ Ranch. In April 2014 the state took possession of the property, saying it had been the site of illegal activities.

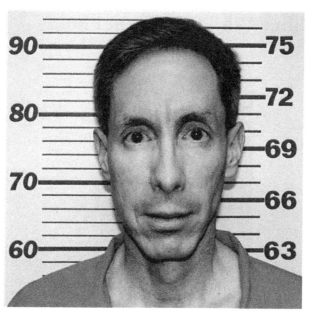

Wanted in Utah and Arizona for various crimes, including sexual conduct with a minor, Warren Jeffs was finally arrested in Las Vegas in 2006.

Killed While She Slept Photos

Lori and Mark Hacking in happier days. She thought he had finished college and been admitted to medical school.

A poster prepared when Lori was found missing. Within a few days, police knew she had not disappeared while jogging, as her husband claimed.

Mark Hacking confessed to family members that he had killed Lori. He was quickly arrested.

If I Die, It May Not Be An Accident Photos

Josh Powell and Susan Cox were married in the Mormon temple in Portland, Ore. in April, 2001. Their reception was at a ward in their hometown of Puyallup the next day

The family looked happy, but by the fall of 2009 Susan was fearful for her life. Photo by Amber Hardman.

After an interview with West Valley City, Utah police, Josh packed up his sons and moved back to Washington State. He never helped search for Susan, and never contacted police to see how the search was going.

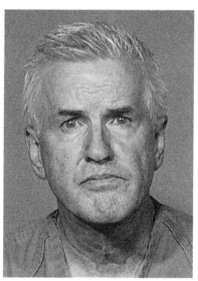

Josh, Charlie, and Braden lived at his father's house until Steve Powell was arrested for voyeurism and pornography in 2011. Steve had been sexually obsessed with his daughter-in-law for years.

Charlie and Braden were temporarily placed with Susan's parents, Chuck and Judy Cox, who hoped to win custody.

After learning that he might never regain custody of his sons and had no power or control left, Josh killed his sons and himself on February 5, 2012.